T0221218

Just Hibernate

Madhusudhan Konda

Beijing · Cambridge · Farnham · Köln · Sebastopol · Tokyo

Just Hibernate

by Madhusudhan Konda

Copyright © 2014 Madhusudhan Konda. All rights reserved.

Printed in the United States of America.

Published by O'Reilly Media, Inc., 1005 Gravenstein Highway North, Sebastopol, CA 95472.

O'Reilly books may be purchased for educational, business, or sales promotional use. Online editions are also available for most titles (*http://my.safaribooksonline.com*). For more information, contact our corporate/institutional sales department: 800-998-9938 or *corporate@oreilly.com*.

Editors: Meghan Blanchette and Brian Anderson	**Indexer:** Ellen Troutman-Zaig
Production Editor: Melanie Yarbrough	**Cover Designer:** Karen Montgomery
Copyeditor: Rachel Monaghan	**Interior Designer:** David Futato
Proofreader: Jasmine Kwityn	**Illustrator:** Rebecca Demarest

June 2014:   First Edition

Revision History for the First Edition:

2014-06-04:   First release

2014-06-27:   Second release

See *http://oreilly.com/catalog/errata.csp?isbn=9781449334376* for release details.

Nutshell Handbook, the Nutshell Handbook logo, and the O'Reilly logo are registered trademarks of O'Reilly Media, Inc. *Just Hibernate*, the cover image of a garden dormouse, and related trade dress are trademarks of O'Reilly Media, Inc.

Many of the designations used by manufacturers and sellers to distinguish their products are claimed as trademarks. Where those designations appear in this book, and O'Reilly Media, Inc. was aware of a trademark claim, the designations have been printed in caps or initial caps.

While every precaution has been taken in the preparation of this book, the publisher and author assume no responsibility for errors or omissions, or for damages resulting from the use of the information contained herein.

ISBN: 978-1-449-33437-6

[LSI]

In memory of my loving Dad; we all miss you!

Table of Contents

Foreword. ix
Preface. xi

1. Basics. 1
   Birth of Hibernate   1
   Problem Domain   3
      MovieManager Application   3
      Improvising the Movie Application   6
   Using Hibernate   8
   Configure the Database Connection   9
   Create Mapping Definitions   10
   Persist the Objects   11
      Creating the Persist Method   12
      Testing the Persisted Data   13
   Setting Up Hibernate   14
   Summary   15

2. Fundamentals. 17
   Object-Relational Mismatch   17
      Inheritance Mismatch   18
      Identity Mismatch   18
      Relations and Associations Mismatch   19
   Hibernate's Main Parts   19
   Persistent Classes   20
   Example: Trading Application   20
   Using Annotations   20
   Configuration   22
      Using a Properties File   22
      Using the XML File   23

Configuration Properties 23
Programmatic Configuration 23
Mapping 24
XML Mapping Files 24
Identifier Generation Strategies 26
Session APIs 27
Transactions 28
Summary 30

3. Annotations. 31
Working Through an Example 31
Digging into Details 33
ID Generation Strategies 34
Composite Identifiers 36
Using Primary Key Class and @Id 36
Using Primary Key Class and @EmbeddedId 37
Using @IdClass 38
Summary 39

4. Persisting Collections. 41
Designing to Interfaces 41
Persisting Lists 42
List Example: Car Showroom 42
Test Client for List Persistence 44
Persisting Sets 45
Persisting Maps 47
Persisting Arrays 49
Persisting Bags and IdBags 50
Persisting Collections Using Annotations 52
Using a Foreign Key 52
Using a Join Table 54
Summary 55

5. Associations. 57
Associations 57
Multiplicity 58
Directionality 59
One-to-One Association 60
Using a Primary Key 61
Testing the Association 63
Using a Foreign Key 64
Annotations 66

One-to-Many (or Many-to-One) Association   67
Bidirectional One-to-Many Association   70
Many-to-Many Association   71
Summary   72

6. **Advanced Concepts**. **73**
   Hibernate Types   73
     Entity and Value Types   73
     Custom Types   74
   Components   75
   Caching   77
     First-Level Caching   77
     Second-Level Caching   78
     Caching Queries   79
   Inheritance Strategies   79
     Table-per-Class Strategy   79
     Table-per-Subclass Strategy   83
     Table-per-Concrete-Class Strategy   85
     Table-per-Concrete-Class Strategy Using XML mapping   85
   Filters   87
     Creating Filter Definitions   87
     Enabling Filters   88
   Relationship Owner (aka Inverse Attribute)   89
   Cascading Entities   89
   Summary   91

7. **Hibernate Query Language**. **93**
   Working with the Query Class   93
     Fetching All Rows   94
     Pagination   96
     Retrieving a Unique Record   96
     Named Parameters   96
     Using the IN option   97
     Positional Parameters   98
     Aliases   98
     Iterators   99
     Selects   99
     Aggregate Functions   100
     Updates and Deletes   101
     Criterias   101
     Named Queries   102
   Native SQL   104

Summary   104

8. Java Persistence API...   105
   Hibernate and JPA   106
      Persistence Context   106
      EntityManagerFactory   108
      EntityManager   109
   Persisting Objects   110
   Saving and Querying Entities   110
   Summary   111

Index...   113

Foreword

One of the great plagues that falls upon Joe/Jane Java Developer is the complex task of mapping their beautifully designed objects onto the world of the Relational Database Management System (RDBMS). Some teams are able to use NoSQL solutions, but for the vast majority of developers, storing data in an RDBMS is a mandatory requirement (often because the database is shared among applications).

Hibernate is the lingua franca of this world, allowing developers to express CRUD operations and complex relationships in the familiar OO language that they know and love. However, as with any technology that attempts to map one paradigm to another (in this case, the object-relational impedance mismatch), there are corner cases and some core information that developers *need* to understand in order to lead sane lives in their day jobs!

Madhu's book covers exactly this, immediately telling you why inheritance, identity, and relations/associations mismatches exist—and *how* to use Hibernate to smoothly deal with them. This book is vital reading for any Java developer, especially in the enterprise space. Madhu has had years of experience in getting this right, and I've seen that work firsthand—it's great to see that finally distilled in this book. Get a copy today!

—Martijn Verburg
CEO of jClarity

Preface

Who Should Read This Book

This book covers the Hibernate framework from the ground up. If you are looking for a short, sweet, and simple introduction to Hibernate, mainly driven by examples, this book is for you. If you have only one weekend to spend learning the framework before starting a Hibernate project on Monday, this book suits you. If you are familiar with the framework but rusty with the details, this is a good refresher!

If you are a seasoned Hibernate developer, this book is probably not for you; it is intended mainly to bring someone up to speed on the technology (but feel free to glance through; you may find something interesting!).

One note of caution: this book is by no means a bible on the Hibernate framework. I tried very hard to condense the material into about 100 pages. If you are looking for really advanced concepts, I wouldn't recommend this book. If you picked up this book to find a solution to your "Hibernate on Mars"—type projects, well, I would say that's a long shot!

Why I Wrote This Book

I believe there are two levels of learning, just like a two-course meal. The first course is a simple and easy one, but creates expectations for an appetizing second course. It not only satisfies our hunger to some extent but also gives us a taste of what's to come in the second course.

Many books offer two-course meals in one go. This is great for many of us. However, in my opinion, we may not have adequate time or space or drive to learn the depths of the technology straightaway. Moreover, as always, we get confused with equally good offerings from different vendors (restaurants, so to speak)! Not to mention, over time, the menus keep changing too!

I believe in serving an appealing, appetizing, and light first-course meal that convinces guests to stay on for the second course. It is a challenging and sometimes daunting task to serve this type of meal!

Working with my seven-year-old son, Joshua, on his homework helped me understand how important (and hard) it is to teach basics and fundamentals in a simple and easy manner. He grasped even the hardest subjects quickly when I got down to his level by explaining them with examples and easy-to-understand language.

I have known many programmers and developers who sometimes stumble on the basics. They often feel shy about asking colleagues for help. I have also met a few who were pushed into projects with new technologies without training or guidance, but were expected to produce results overnight.

There are people who are genuinely interested in learning the technology but may be put off by the big texts or manuals. These people are enthusiastic and want to hit the ground running, but they don't have the time or patience to read and digest volumes of data! They have time only to read a simple book, learn the technology, and jump straight into practice. Once they get the hang of it, their grey matter will ask for more and more.

When I want to learn something new, I start experimenting with basic code, move an inch further, burn a bit of code, and so on. Once I get a feel for the framework, I turn to other avenues to quench my thirst. At that point, I seek out the advanced, in-depth manuals and specs, and of course, the big books.

My motive behind the *Just* series of books is to deliver simple yet powerful page-turners. I aim to deliver straight-to-the-point, no-nonsense, and example-driven books on my favorite technologies. And, of course, I'd like them to be easy reads. These books should give you enough knowledge and confidence to start working on real-world projects.

How This Book Is Organized

The book is presented in eight simple chapters. Each chapter will deal with one or two specific themes. All the chapters are presented with code snippets to illustrate the technology in detail. You should download and work closely with the accompanying source code.

The organization and goals of the chapters are as follows:

Chapter 1, Basics

> This chapter sets the scene for using Hibernate. We define the problem domain, work out a solution using JDBC, and reengineer the problem employing Hibernate. We'll get a taste of the framework from a very high level.

Chapter 2, Fundamentals

You learned about the problem Hibernate is trying to solve in the first chapter. Here, in the second chapter, we dive into the framework to explore its moving parts and their work in action. We walk through Hibernate's fundamental pieces in detail.

Chapter 3, Annotations

In this chapter, we will focus on creating Hibernate applications using annotations. This chapter covers the basics of annotations, getting you ready to jump into the Hibernate annotations that we'll be using in the rest of the book.

Chapter 4, Persisting Collections

Persisting collections is a challenging task for developers. This chapter is dedicated to helping you understand the mechanics of persistence and how to work with collections.

Chapter 5, Associations

You'll learn about Hibernate's support for associations and relationships in this chapter. It covers the fundamental associations, such as one-to-many and many-to-many, with relevant examples. I tried to keep this chapter as slim as possible, but given the extent of the relevant material, I slightly missed my target! This is an important chapter, and getting associations right is half your job done!

Chapter 6, Advanced Concepts

This chapter deals with a few advanced concepts such as caching, inheritance strategies, types, and filters. You should run through this chapter to gain a better understanding of the framework and what it provides in relation to inheritance, caching, and other features.

Chapter 7, Hibernate Query Language

Similar to SQL, Hibernate exposes its own query language to work with objects. This chapter introduces you to HQL and walks you through the API with examples.

Chapter 8, Java Persistence API

This chapter looks at a standard in the Java Persistence world, JPA, from Hibernate's view. We discuss Hibernate's support in implementing JPA standards and how we can use them in our applications.

Conventions Used in This Book

The following typographical conventions are used in this book:

Italic

Indicates new terms, URLs, email addresses, filenames, and file extensions.

`Constant width`

> Used for program listings, as well as within paragraphs to refer to program elements such as variable or function names, databases, data types, environment variables, statements, and keywords.

`Constant width bold`

> Shows commands or other text that should be typed literally by the user.

`Constant width italic`

> Shows text that should be replaced with user-supplied values or by values determined by context.

 This element signifies a tip or suggestion.

 This element signifies a general note.

 This element indicates a warning or caution.

Using Code Examples

Supplemental material (code examples, exercises, etc.) is available for download at *https://github.com/madhusudhankonda/jh.git*.

This book is here to help you get your job done. In general, if example code is offered with this book, you may use it in your programs and documentation. You do not need to contact us for permission unless you're reproducing a significant portion of the code. For example, writing a program that uses several chunks of code from this book does not require permission. Selling or distributing a CD-ROM of examples from O'Reilly books does require permission. Answering a question by citing this book and quoting example code does not require permission. Incorporating a significant amount of example code from this book into your product's documentation does require permission.

We appreciate, but do not require, attribution. An attribution usually includes the title, author, publisher, and ISBN. For example: "*Just Hibernate* by Madhusudhan Konda (O'Reilly), Copyright 2014 Madhusudhan Konda, 978-1-449-33437-6."

If you feel your use of code examples falls outside fair use or the permission given above, feel free to contact us at *permissions@oreilly.com*.

Safari® Books Online

 Safari Books Online is an on-demand digital library that delivers expert content in both book and video form from the world's leading authors in technology and business.

Technology professionals, software developers, web designers, and business and creative professionals use Safari Books Online as their primary resource for research, problem solving, learning, and certification training.

Safari Books Online offers a range of product mixes and pricing programs for organizations, government agencies, and individuals. Subscribers have access to thousands of books, training videos, and prepublication manuscripts in one fully searchable database from publishers like O'Reilly Media, Prentice Hall Professional, Addison-Wesley Professional, Microsoft Press, Sams, Que, Peachpit Press, Focal Press, Cisco Press, John Wiley & Sons, Syngress, Morgan Kaufmann, IBM Redbooks, Packt, Adobe Press, FT Press, Apress, Manning, New Riders, McGraw-Hill, Jones & Bartlett, Course Technology, and dozens more. For more information about Safari Books Online, please visit us online.

How to Contact Us

Please address comments and questions concerning this book to the publisher:

O'Reilly Media, Inc.
1005 Gravenstein Highway North
Sebastopol, CA 95472
800-998-9938 (in the United States or Canada)
707-829-0515 (international or local)
707-829-0104 (fax)

We have a web page for this book, where we list errata, examples, and any additional information. You can access this page at *http://bit.ly/just-hibernate*.

To comment or ask technical questions about this book, send email to *bookquestions@oreilly.com*.

For more information about our books, courses, conferences, and news, see our website at *http://www.oreilly.com*.

Find us on Facebook: *http://facebook.com/oreilly*

Follow us on Twitter: *http://twitter.com/oreillymedia*

Watch us on YouTube: *http://www.youtube.com/oreillymedia*

Acknowledgments

Without my family, this book wouldn't have seen light. Without the O'Reilly team (Mike, Meghan, Brian, Rachel, Melanie, and Jasmine), this project wouldn't have been fruitful. Without my friends (Trevor, Hitesh, Biswo, and others), I wouldn't have a beautiful script! Last but not least, it is *you*, the reader, who made me write more. I am certainly thrilled to provide yet another "Just" book for you! Without appreciation, I wouldn't be writing this book!

I sincerely thank you all for helping me out in this endeavor!

A Note from the Author

I have received positive and negative (I certainly take it as constructive) feedback, reviews, comments, suggestions, and praise for my other books, which has certainly encouraged me to do more. If my writings haven't lived up to your expectations, let me know and I will try my best next time. As my son Joshua says, "A good man never gives up, Dad!" I will not give up!

I hope you enjoy reading this as much as I have enjoyed writing it!

Please get in touch with me, even if you don't like me or my writing. :) Your feedback always helps me. If you are in and around London, do ping me so I may join you for a coffee or a cake!

Other *Just XXX* (the next one is *Just Java8*) books will be on their way, so stay tuned.

Yours sincerely,
Madhusudhan Konda
www.madhusudhan.com
m.konda@outlook.com
@mkonda007 (*https://twitter.com/mkonda007*)

CHAPTER 1

Basics

There are two different software worlds: one is the Java world, where none other than objects are known, while the other is the relational database world, where data is king.

Java developers always work with objects that represent state and behavior modeling real-world problems. Object *persistence* is a fundamental requirement of Java applications. The state is modeled to be persisted in durable storage so it will be permanent.

On the other hand, when it is time to store the data, we have to rely on relational databases, where the data is traditionally represented in a row-column format with relationships and associations. Bringing Java objects to the relational world is always a challenging and complex task for Java developers. This process is often referred to as *object-relational mapping* (ORM).

This chapter sets the tone for our Hibernate discussion by first looking at the problem domain of object persistence. We will explore the technologies and tools, such as JDBC and Hibernate, that assist us in facing this challenge. We will compare and contrast both of these technologies and learn how Hibernate achieves object-relational-model persistence with ease and comfort.

Birth of Hibernate

Say we are designing an online banking system. We expect the bank to keep a safe copy of our accounts, personal details, preferences, and transactions. This means, in order to be durable, the application data must be persisted to a permanent storage space. In the context of this bank application, by persistent data I mean the customer, address, account, and other domain objects that we may have modeled in our design. The data that's been persisted by our application will outlive the application itself—for example, we may have moved away from online to phone banking, but the data created by our bank application should still be visible or available if required.

So, we know now that persisting the objects (their state is the data that we need to persist) is a fundamental requirement for most real-world applications. To save the data, we need durable storage spaces called databases. There are a plethora of database vendors (such as Oracle, MySQL, DB2, JavaDB, and others) with a lengthy list of bells and whistles.

How can we persist an object graph to a database?

Enterprises employ object-oriented languages (such as Java) as their programming platforms and relational databases (such as Oracle, MySQL, Sybase, etc.) for data storage. The existence of these two software technologies is a must for most real-world applications in spite of the so-called "object-relational impedance mismatch." We will discuss the mismatch in the next chapter in detail, but to give you an introduction, I'll explain its main points here:

- Inheritance is the fundamental object-oriented programming principle without which object associations would be impossible to design. Databases do not understand inheritance!

- When it comes to the rich set of object associations like one-to-one, one-to-many, and many-to-many, databases fall flat, as they cannot support all types of relationships.

- Lastly, there is also an identity mismatch: objects carry both an identity and equality, while database records are identified with their column values.

Developers mitigate these differences by employing various home-grown frameworks and other technical solutions and strategies.

Java has a standard tool set for accessing databases. It is called the Java Database Connectivity (JDBC) application programming interface (API). The API was very well used in Java applications until recently. While the API is well suited for small projects, it becomes quite cumbersome (and sometimes out of hand) as the domain model increases in complexity. The API also includes a lot of repetitive boilerplate code, requiring the developer to do a lot of manual coding. Furthermore, handling of the object-relational model mapping is heavy-handed too!

This was the pain point for developers: we all wished for a simple tool to persist the data without so much hassle. The Hibernate team found the gaps in the ORM mapping space and took advantage by creating a simple framework that would make the developer's life easy.

That's when Hibernate was born! Hibernate became an instant hit and is undeniably the most popular open source tool in the ORM tools domain. The framework was embraced overnight by the community for its simplicity and powerful features.

Problem Domain

Before we jump into exploring Hibernate in detail, let's look at an example of the type of problem that Hibernate was invented to solve.

We all (well, at least most of us!) love watching movies. Obviously, we don't have all the time in the world to watch those movies when they hit the screen. So we create a "wish list" of movies that we would like to watch. For this reason, we wake up one fine morning and decide to write a simple application called JustMovies! It is a web-based application that allows users to sign up for their own account to create their movie wish list. They can return to the website any time to add, modify, or delete the movies in their wish list. As we have to store the list of each user, it is imperative that we store this wish list in durable storage such as a database.

Let's first create a simple Java application that would store and retrieve movies from a database.

MovieManager Application

Consider a Java application called `MovieManager` whose main job is to save, find, and retrieve the movies from a database. In addition to coding the Java application, we need a database table to store the movie information. This `MOVIES` table will store the data about movies as rows, as shown in Table 1-1.

Table 1-1. MOVIES

ID	TITLE	DIRECTOR	SYNOPSIS
1	Top Gun	Tony Scott	When Maverick encounters a pair of MiGs…
2	Jaws	Steven Spielberg	A tale of a white shark!

Each row will represent a `Movie` instance in our `VanillaMovieManager` application.

Let's pretend we live in a world without Hibernate. We'll write some sample code using JDBC that will, hopefully, meet our requirements.

Using JDBC

The first step in any database application is to establish a connection with the database. A connection is a gateway to the database for carrying out the operations on the data from a Java application. JDBC provides a connection API to create connections based on the database properties that we provide. Database providers typically implement a class that holds the database connection mechanism—for example, for the MySQL database, this class is `com.mysql.jdbc.Driver` and for the JavaDB (derby) database it's `org.apache.derby.jdbc.EmbeddedDriver`.

Note that we use the MySQL database throughout the book. Refer to "Setting Up Hibernate" on page 14 for details on how to set up the project and database.

The `createConnection` method, shown in the following snippet, demonstrates the procedure to create a database connection:

```
public class VanillaMovieManager {
  private Connection connection = null;

  // Database properties
  private String url = "jdbc:mysql://localhost:3307/JH";
  private String driverClass = "com.mysql.jdbc.Driver";
  private String username = "mkonda";
  private String password = "mypass";
  ...
  private Connection getConnection() {
    try {
        Class.forName(driverClass).newInstance();
        connection = DriverManager.getConnection(url, username, password);
    } catch (Exception ex) {
        System.err.println("Exception:"+ ex.getMessage());
    }
    return connection;
  }
}
```

In this snippet, we first instantiate the driver class, and then get a connection using the `DriverManager`.

Once we have established our connection to the database successfully, our next step is to write a method to persist and query a `Movie` entity. Most parts of the methods should be familiar if you have had any experience with JDBC code.

Continuing with our application development, let's add a couple of methods that will save the movies to and retrieve them from the database. We call these methods as `persistMovie` and `queryMovies`, respectively. The implementation of these methods is shown in the following code listing:

```
public class VanillaMovieManager {
  private String insertSql = "INSERT INTO MOVIES VALUES (?,?,?,?)";
  private String selectSql = "SELECT * FROM MOVIES";
  ...
  private void persistMovie() {
    try {
        PreparedStatement pst = getConnection().prepareStatement(insertSql);
        pst.setInt(1, 1001);
        pst.setString(2, "Top Gun");
```

```
                pst.setString(3, "Action Film");
                pst.setString(4, "Tony Scott");

                // Execute the statement
            pst.execute();
                System.out.println("Movie persisted successfully!");

            } catch (SQLException ex) {
                System.err.println(ex.getMessage());
                ex.printStackTrace();
            }
    }
    private void queryMovies() {
        try {
            Statement st = getConnection().createStatement();
            ResultSet rs = st.executeQuery("SELECT * FROM MOVIES");
            while (rs.next()) {
                System.out.println("Movie Found: "
                        + rs.getInt("ID")
                        + ", Title:"
                        + rs.getString("TITLE"));
            }
        } catch (SQLException ex) {
            System.err.println(ex.getMessage());
            }
        }
    }
}
```

This is what we've done in the preceding example code:

1. We've created a `PreparedStatement` from the connection with the `insertSql` string.

2. We've set the statement with values (column values against column numbers: 1 is ID, 2 is title, etc.).

3. We've executed the statement that should insert the movie in the table.

4. We've queried the database for all `Movies` and printed them out to the console.

The steps are pretty much self-explanatory. We create a `PreparedStatement` and execute it after setting the appropriate values on it for each column. Once we know that the execution worked, we query the database with a `SELECT` statement in order to fetch all the movies available and print them to the console.

However, there are a few things to note:

- We use a predefined SQL statement to insert (or select) column values.

- We set the column values one by one using the position number (or column name).

- We catch the `SQLException` if the code misbehaves.

For simple programs, this way of creating the statements with the values and executing them is fine. However, the kinds of programs we have to deal with in the real world are much more complex. JDBC will work, if you are willing and able to write and manage a great deal of nonbusiness code. Also, using JDBC might pose a challenge when you have a lot of tables or complex relationships between the objects. We are not dealing with the data in any shape or form using our favorite object orientation principles!

Improvising the Movie Application

Wouldn't it be ideal to call a method such as `persist()` on a utility class so that the `Movie` object is persisted straightaway? After all, we are object-oriented programmers; wishing for this facility is not a sin!

To achieve this goal, we will create a *plain old Java object* (POJO) representing a movie. For every celluloid movie that's released (or yet to be released), we'll have a new `Movie` object created. The `Movie` POJO is defined here:

```
public class Movie {
  private int id = 0;
  private String  title = null;
  private String  synopsis = null;
  private String  director = null;
  ...
  // Setters and getters omitted
}
```

So, all we need now is for a facility to persist this POJO object into our database table `MOVIES`—in essence converting the object model (`Movie` object) to a relational model (table row).

Let's create a `MoviePersistor` class that might do this job:

```
// Pseudocode
public class MoviePersistor {
  public void persist(Movie movie) {
      // Persisting a movie goes here
  }
  public void fetch(String title) {
      // Fetching a movie by title goes here
  }
  ...
}
```

We haven't written the `persist` or `fetch` functionality yet; that's not the theme of the program. Now let's see how easy it is to persist any `Movie` using the `MoviePersistor` utility class, as demonstrated in this sample test:

```
//Pseudocode
MoviePersistor moviePersistor = new MoviePersistor();
Movie movie = new Movie();
movie.setId(1);
movie.setTitle("Jaws");
movie.setDirector("Steven Spielberg");
movie.setSynopsis("Story of a great white shark!");

moviePersistor.persist(movie);
```

How cool is that? A POJO representing a celluloid movie is persisted as a row of records into a database table—object model to relational model—via a utility class!

That's all good, except for the actual `persist` and `fetch` method implementations. To implement this functionality, we not only need the connection facility to a database, we also need a mechanism to convert the object to a row (such as mapping our object properties to database columns).

We could write our own framework of classes to hide the nitty-gritty of these conversions and persistence mechanisms (which may use good old JDBC statements behind the scenes). Although writing this framework isn't rocket science, it would be a time-consuming and cumbersome effort to begin with.

Over time, an organization's persistence requirements may change or it may even migrate the database from, for example, Oracle to MySQL. This means the framework would have to be very generic and account for a plethora of functional and technical requirements before hitting the ground.

In my experience, such homegrown frameworks are unmanageable, inflexible, unscalable, and sometimes out of date too! Unless the requirement is really dead-specific to an organization (your organization may want to persist data to Mars!), I would strongly recommend that you search on the Internet to choose one that closely satisfies our predicates.

But before you go on your way to start writing this code, let me be the bearer of some good news (if you haven't already have heard this): there's already a great framework that does exactly this—object persistence to a relational database—called *Hibernate*!

Now that we've got a persistence framework, let's see how the same method that persists our movie can be refactored through Hibernate:

```
public class BasicMovieManager {
    private void persistMovie(Movie movie) {
        Session session = sessionFactory.getCurrentSession();
        ...
        session.save(movie);
    }
    ...
}
```

Did you notice that we saved the `Movie` instance to a database by a executing a single line of code: `session.save(movie)`? Isn't this what we had wished for earlier—a class that would simply save the persistent objects in an object-oriented way? Hibernate's API classes expose several methods to manipulate the Java objects with ease and comfort. We neither have to write reams of code using JDBC nor fold up our sleeves and write a framework while scratching our heads and gulping gallons of caffeine!

Hibernate does provide the capability of object persistence; however, there is a one-off configuration and mapping we need to let Hibernate know our intentions. We delve into these details at a very high level in next couple of sections.

Using Hibernate

The standard steps to follow in creating a Hibernate application are:

1. Configure the database connection.
2. Create mapping definitions.
3. Persist the classes.

Here are the common steps involved in developing the Java-Hibernate version of our `MovieManager` application:

1. Create a `Movie` domain object (domain model POJOs representing data tables).
2. Create configuration files such as Hibernate properties and mapping files.
3. Create a test client that manages (insert/update/delete/find) the `Movies`.

We have already prepared a `Movie` POJO, as shown in prior snippets, so we don't have to go over it again.

The heart of any Hibernate application is in its configuration. There are two pieces of configuration required in any Hibernate application: one creates the database connections, and the other creates the object-to-table mapping. As with JDBC, we need to provide the database information to our application so it will open up a connection for manipulating the data. The mapping configuration defines which object properties are mapped to which columns of the table. We are not going to go into detail about them here, as the aim of this chapter is to get you started quickly!

Let's look at the standard steps for creating a Hibernate application in the following sections.

Configure the Database Connection

To create a connection to the database, Hibernate must know the details of our database, tables, classes, and other mechanics. This information is ideally provided as an XML file (usually named *hibernate.cfg.xml*) or as a simple text file with name/value pairs (usually named *hibernate.properties*).

For this exercise, we use XML style. We name this file *hibernate.cfg.xml* so the framework can load this file automatically.

The following snippet describes such a configuration file. Because I am using MySQL as the database, the connection details for the MySQL database are declared in this *hibernate.cfg.xml* file:

```
<hibernate-configuration>
  <session-factory>
    <property name="connection.url">
        jdbc:mysql://localhost:3307/JH
        </property>
    <property name="connection.driver_class">
        com.mysql.jdbc.Driver
        </property>
    <property name="connection.username">
        mkonda
        </property>
    <property name="connection.password">
        password
        </property>
    <property name="dialect">
        org.hibernate.dialect.MySQL5Dialect
        </property>
    <mapping resource="Movie.hbm.xml" />
  </session-factory>
</hibernate-configuration>
```

This file has enough information to get a live connection to a MySQL database.

The preceding properties can also be expressed as name/value pairs. For example, here's the same information represented as name/value pairs in a text file titled *hibernate.properties*:

```
hibernate.connection.driver_class = com.mysql.jdbc.Driver
hibernate.connection.url = jdbc:mysql://localhost:3307/JH
hibernate.dialect = org.hibernate.dialect.MySQL5Dialect
```

`connection.url` indicates the URL to which we should be connected, `driver_class` represents the relevant `Driver` class to make a connection, and the dialect indicates which database dialect we are using (MySQL, in this case).

If you are following the *hibernate.properties* file approach, note that all the properties are prefixed with "hibernate" and follow a pattern—*hibernate.* properties*, for instance.

Beyond providing the configuration properties, we also have to provide mapping files and their locations. As mentioned earlier, a mapping file indicates the mapping of object properties to the row column values. This mapping is done in a separate file, usually suffixed with *.hbm.xml*. We must let Hibernate know our mapping definition files by including an element `mapping` property in the previous config file, as shown here:

```
<hibernate-configuration>
  <session-factory>
    ...
    <mapping resource="Movie.hbm.xml" />
        <mapping resource="Account.hbm.xml" />
        <mapping resource="Trade.hbm.xml" />
  </session-factory>
</hibernate-configuration>
```

The `resource` attribute indicates the name of the mapping resource that Hibernate should load. In this case, *Movie.hbm.xml* is the mapping file and consists of details on how a `Movie` object is mapped to a `MOVIE` table. You can see others as well, such as *Account.hbm.xml* and *Trade.hbm.xml*. We will look at these mapping files in a minute.

What does Hibernate do with this properties file?

The Hibernate framework loads this file to create a `SessionFactory`, which is a thread-safe global factory class for creating `Sessions`. We should ideally create a single `SessionFactory` and share it across the application. Note that a `SessionFactory` is defined for one, and only one, database. For instance, if you have another database alongside MySQL, you should define the relevant configuration in *hibernate.hbm.xml* to create a separate `SessionFactory` for that database too.

The goal of the `SessionFactory` is to create `Session` objects. `Session` is a gateway to our database. It is the `Session`'s job to take care of all database operations such as saving, loading, and retrieving records from relevant tables. The framework also maintains a transactional medium around our application. The operations involving the database access are wrapped up in a single unit of work called a *transaction*. So, all the operations in that transaction are either successful or rolled back.

Keep in mind that the configuration is used to create a `Session` via a `SessionFactory` instance. Before we move on, note that `Session` objects are not thread-safe and therefore should not be shared across different classes. We will see the details of how they should be used as we progress in this book.

Create Mapping Definitions

Once we have the connection configuration ready, the next step is to prepare the *Movie.hbm.xml* file consisting of object-table mapping definitions. The following XML snippet defines mapping for our `Movie` object against the `MOVIES` table:

```xml
<hibernate-mapping>
  <class name="com.madhusudhan.jh.domain.Movie" table="MOVIES">
    <id name="id" column="ID">
        <generator class="native"/>
    </id>
    <property name="title" column="TITLE"/>
    <property name="director" column="DIRECTOR"/>
    <property name="synopsis" column="SYNOPSIS"/>
  </class>
</hibernate-mapping>
```

There is a lot going on in this mapping file. The hibernate-mapping element holds all the class-to-table mapping definitions. Individual mappings per object are declared under the class element. The name attribute of the class tag refers to our POJO domain class com.madhusudhan.jh.domain.Movie, while the table attribute refers to the table MOVIES to which the objects are persisted.

The remaining properties indicate the mapping from the object's variables to the table's columns (e.g., the id is mapped to ID, the title to TITLE, director to DIRECTOR, etc.). Each object must have a unique identifier—similar to a primary key on the table. We set this identifier by implementing the id tag using a native strategy. Don't pay too much attention to this id and the generation strategy yet. We will discuss them in detail in the coming chapters.

Persist the Objects

Now that the configuration is out of our way, let's create a client that persists the objects with the help of Hibernate.

We need the SessionFactory instance from which we create a Session object. The following snippet shows the initial setup for creating the SessionFactory class:

```java
public class BasicMovieManager {
  private SessionFactory sessionFactory = null;

  // Creating SessionFactory using 4.2 version of Hibernate
  private void initSessionFactory(){
   Configuration config = new Configuration().configure();
    // Build a Registry with our configuration properties
   ServiceRegistry serviceRegistry = new ServiceRegistryBuilder().applySettings(
       config.getProperties()).buildServiceRegistry();

    // create the session factory
   sessionFactory = config.buildSessionFactory(serviceRegistry);
  }
  ...
}
```

Note that we don't have to explicitly mention the mapping or configuration or properties files, because the Hibernate runtime looks for default filenames, such as *hibernate.cfg.xml* or *hibernate.properties*, in the classpath and loads them. If we have a non-default name, make sure you pass that as an argument—like `configure("my-hib-cfg.xml")`, for example.

The preceding settings for initializing the `SessionFactory` class are for the latest Hibernate version at the time of this writing, 4.2. The Hibernate 4.x version introduced service registries, which we will see in later chapters.

 In 3.x versions, the `configure` method rummages through the classpath looking for a file named *hibernate.cfg.xml* (or *hibernate.properties*) to create a `Configuration` object. This configuration object is then used to create a `SessionFactory` instance. If you are using a pre-4.x version of Hibernate, use the following code to initialize the `SessionFactory`:

```
//Creating SessionFactory using 3.x version of Hibernate
private void init3x(){
    sessionFactory =
        new Configuration().configure().buildSessionFactory();
}
```

In 4.x versions, this is slightly modified by the introduction `Service Registry`, which takes a `Map` of properties that can be fed from a `Configuration` object, as just shown.

Whichever version you choose, the `SessionFactory` thus created is the same and so are the `Sessions`.

Creating the Persist Method

Now on to the actual workings of the `BasicMovieManager` class. The persist method is defined on the class to persist a movie using `Session`'s `save` method. This is shown in the following snippet:

```
public class BasicMovieManager {
  private void persistMovie(Movie movie) {
      Session session = sessionFactory.getCurrentSession();
      session.beginTransaction();
      session.save(movie);
      session.getTransaction().commit();
  }
}
```

It looks simple, doesn't it? We did not write unnecessary or repetitious code at all, but concentrated on the business function of saving the object.

In the preceding snippet, we first grab a `Session` from the factory. We then create a transaction object (we'll learn more about transactions in later chapters), and persist the incoming `Movie` object using the `session.save` method. Finally, we commit the transaction, and the `Movie` is stored permanently in our database.

Testing the Persisted Data

We have two ways of testing the persisted data: running a native SQL query on the database, or creating a test client.

We can run the SQL query on the database using something like `SELECT * FROM MOVIES`, which fetches all the records stored by our application.

The SQL select query prints the output as shown in Table 1-2.

Table 1-2. MOVIES

ID	TITLE	DIRECTOR	SYNOPSIS
1	Top Gun	Tony Scott	Maverick is a hot pilot…
2	Jaws	Steven Spielberg	A tale of a white shark!

Alternatively, we can create another method in our test client, say `findMovie`. This method will use the `Session`'s `load` method to fetch the record from the database. We invoke the `findMovie` method, passing the movie ID as the argument, to fetch the movie:

```
public class BasicMovieManager {
   ...
   private void findMovie(int movieId) {
        Session session = sessionFactory.getCurrentSession();
        session.beginTransaction();

        Movie movie = (Movie)session.load(Movie.class, movieId);

        System.out.println("Movie:"+movie);
        session.getTransaction().commit();
   }
}
```

The `load` method on the `Session` API fetches the appropriate `Movie` object for a given identifier. If you are thinking that Hibernate may use a `SELECT` statement behind the scenes, you are correct!

Should you wish to fetch *all* movies from the table, you create a `Query` object with the simple query string `"from Movie"` and execute it. The `list` method on the query (created via `session.createQuery`) returns a `List` of movies, as shown here:

```
public class BasicMovieManager {
   // Finding all movies
   private void findAll() {
```

```
    Session session = sessionFactory.getCurrentSession();
        session.beginTransaction();
        List<Movie> movies = session.createQuery("from Movie").list();*
        session.getTransaction().commit();
    System.out.println("All Movies:"+movies);
    }
    ...
}
```

Setting Up Hibernate

Setting up a Hibernate project is easy. The project that I've prepared for this book is a Maven-based code developed on NetBeans IDE. I won't be going into detail on setting up the environment, but the following steps should help you. Although I have used NetBeans for developing code, you can use any of your favorite IDEs to work on this project. Also, you can swap MySQL with any other databases, including in-memory ones such as Derby or HyperSQL.

First, you should set up the essential development environment consisting of JDK 5.0+, NetBeans IDE, Maven, and the MySQL database (you may have had this environment already!). I have used JDK 6, NetBeans 7.3, Maven 3.2, and MySQL 5.2 for developing the code, and the Hibernate version is 4.2.3.Final.

Once you have the dev environment sorted, the next step is to create a Maven project in NetBeans (or Eclipse). Add the appropriate Hibernate dependencies to the *pom.xml* file as shown here:

```
<project xmlns="http://maven.apache.org/POM/4.0.0"
  xmlns:xsi="http://www.w3.org/2001/XMLSchema-instance"
    xsi:schemaLocation="http://maven.apache.org/POM/4.0.0
    http://maven.apache.org/xsd/maven-4.0.0.xsd">
  <modelVersion>4.0.0</modelVersion>
  <groupId>com.madhusudhan</groupId>
  <artifactId>just-hibernate</artifactId>
  <version>0.0.1-SNAPSHOT</version>
  <dependencies>
    <dependency>
      <groupId>org.hibernate</groupId>
      <artifactId>hibernate-core</artifactId>
      <version>4.2.3.Final</version>
    </dependency>
    <dependency>
      <groupId>mysql</groupId>
      <artifactId>mysql-connector-java</artifactId>
      <version>5.1.18</version>
    </dependency>
    ...
  </project>
```

Maven will resolve the related dependencies when building the project. I recommend downloading the book's source code and importing the project into your favorite IDE.

The next step is setting up your database. If you already have a database, you can skip this step. I am using MySQL database. Download the latest MySQL package and install it on your machine (you may have to go through the manual to set this up correctly). You can try out the examples in this book using any other databases.

Once you have MySQL (or any other database) installed, make sure you create a schema named JH, as shown here:

```
CREATE SCHEMA JH;
```

Most of the tables in this project were autogenerated by Hibernate; that is, Hibernate would create them on the fly (if they do not exist) by reading your configuration. We need to set a property, hbm2ddl.auto, in the Hibernate configuration file (*hibernate.cfg.xml*) to the appropriate value for this autogeneration to happen, as follows:

```
<property name="hbm2ddl.auto">update</property>
```

When we set this property, the tables are automatically either created if they do not exist or updated if there's a change in the table schema.

 Never use the hbm2ddl.auto property in production! You must create a schema with all the table definitions and deploy to production via a proper release process.

That's pretty much it!

We wished for a mechanism that hides away the nitty-gritty of clumsy JDBC statements and connections. We dreamed of creating facility methods that would store a POJO object directly to the database without the hassle of setting/getting the columns. We've fulfilled our dreams and wishes by embracing Hibernate!

You may have lots of questions, but they'll be demystified as we go through our journey, so stay tuned in!

Summary

In this chapter, we learned about the object-relational-model problem domain by walking through an example. Although we can use JDBC for data access, we found that it requires a lot of manual mapping and unnecessarily repetitive code. We took a small step and introduced Hibernate to solve the problem of object-to-relational data persistence. From a high level, we took a look at the Hibernate concepts of SessionFactory and `Sessions`. We refactored the JDBC example to use the Hibernate framework and successfully persisted and queried the POJOs as expected.

In the next chapter, we'll go through the fundamentals of Hibernate in detail.

CHAPTER 2

Fundamentals

In the previous chapter, we walked through a basic example of persisting Movie objects using the Hibernate framework. We skipped over the details, as our aim was to get a quick taste of Hibernate without having to worry about the ingredients. Now is the time to learn the fundamentals of the framework to cement these foundations. This chapter deals with such fundamentals.

But before we go into those Hibernate details, there's one thing you should understand first: the core problem of the object-relational model mismatch (which is the very reason why ORM was developed in the first place).

Object-Relational Mismatch

In an object-relational persistence world, no discussion would be complete without a grasp of the object-relational paradigm mismatch. Understanding this paradigm will give you some insight into the inception and existence of ORM tools.

The object world is designed to solve specific problems: booking a flight, transferring money, shopping for books, and so on. Technical solutions are designed with a *domain model* in mind to solve these problems. The domain model defines the objects representing a real-world problem. A flight reservation, bank account, and book search are examples of *domain objects*. These domain objects are expected to be stored and retrieved from a database.

Most of the real-world applications cannot exist without some form of persistence. We would go crazy if our banks said that they lost our money because they hadn't stored our deposits in a durable storage space. We would be very angry with the airline if we bought a ticket but found out we were not booked on the plane the day we're supposed to fly out for a holiday. Of all the choices available, relational database persistence is the industry standard of durable storage.

Relational databases store the data in a two-dimensional format: rows and columns. The data relationships are expressed in the form of foreign keys.

The problem arises when we start thinking of storing the domain objects into a relational database. The objects in our application are not in a row-column format; they hold state using attributes (variables). So, unfortunately, they can't be stored as is. At a very high level, this mismatch is called *object-relational impedance mismatch*.

There are a few fundamental differences between the object and relational models, which are discussed briefly here.

Inheritance Mismatch

The major (object-oriented) feature that the object world supports and relational schemas do not is *inheritance*. As we all know, this is the bread and butter of any object-oriented language (Java in particular). Unfortunately, the relational schema does not know anything about inheritance.

Take an example of an employee and an executive: each executive *is an* employee. Representing this *is a* relationship in the database isn't a clear-cut exercise, as it requires tweaking the table relationships. We know how important inheritance is to a Java programmer; without it, designing for real-world problems would be too messy. The database does not understand these types of associations. There is no straightforward solution; however, there are a few approaches to solving this problem. These approaches employ various class-to-table strategies, which we will see in later chapters. Note that *has a* relations are expressed in the database, though.

Identity Mismatch

The objects in a Java application, for example, have both identity and equality. For example, see the definition of the Trade POJO described here:

```
public class Trade {
  private long tradeId = -1;
  private double quantity = 0;
  private String security = null;
  ...
```

Two objects represent the same memory location, so they are treated as identical:

```
Trade trade1 = new Trade();
Trade trade2 = trade1;

// Memory location is identical—identity check!
if(trade1==trade2){..}

// Values are identical—equality check!
if(trade1.equals(trade2)){..}
```

When we are comparing the trades using the == operator, we are comparing based on the memory location. This check will compare the memory addresses of two trade objects, and if they have the same address (like `trade1` and `trade2`), they are *identical*.

On the other hand, if the values of an object (`trade1`) are equal to another (`trade2`) object, we say these objects are *equal*. In the preceding example, the second `if` block using the `equals` method indicates this. As developers, we are responsible for writing a valid `equals` method.

In the Java world, we know the difference between using == versus `equals`: we use == for identity checking and the `equals` method for equality.

In a relational schema, however, there are no identity and equality concepts. The rows (or records) are identified with their values in the columns. To overcome the identity and equality feature deficiencies, databases tend to employ *primary key* strategies. These primary key identifiers, which represent individual rows, are then modeled as one of the object properties to bridge the gap. For example, the trade's `tradeId` attribute will be mapped to a `TRADE_ID` primary key on the `TRADES` table.

Relations and Associations Mismatch

In object-oriented programming languages like Java, *associations* are a key feature. In the real world, a shopping basket is a collection of items; a car has properties such as registration, make and model, and specific engine; `Trade` has an instrument, volume, and maturity date. In Java, these relationships are all expressed as some form of association. Normally, we do expect a very rich set of associations in a Java application.

The good thing is that these associations are supported by relational databases to some extent. The foreign key referring to a primary key of another table is the way of expressing an association in a relational schema. However, object models (in Java) exhibit not just one but three types of associations: one-to-one, one-to-many (or many-to-one), and many-to-many. Converting these associations to a foreign key/primary key association is a challenging task, although not impossible.

The birth of ORM tools was not accidental; they were born out of necessity. Bridging the gap between the object and relational models was a laborious process that posed numerous challenges. ORM tools such as Hibernate were developed to automate the object-relational persistence strategies.

Hibernate's Main Parts

At a broad level, there are three important pieces across all Hibernate applications:

- Persistent classes (our POJOs and AJOs [annotated Java objects!])
- Configuration and mapping definitions

- Access and manipulation of the data using the API

Our domain model is a representation of object persistence. The domain objects are modeled as persistent classes (or entities) in our application. The configuration tells us which objects are to be stored and where they should be persisted. Lastly, we use Hibernate's API to fetch, save, delete, and update the data.

We will go through these moving parts in detail in the coming sections.

Persistent Classes

The fundamental requirement of a business application is that the data survives the application that created it. For instance, in our JustMovies! application, a `Movie` object modeled to represent a movie can be accessed even if the application that created it ceases to exist.

We can fulfill this requirement of durable objects by creating domain objects (POJOs and AJOs) and using Hibernate to persist them in a durable storage space. Creating these objects for persistence is straightforward, as we'll see next.

Example: Trading Application

Let's consider a Java application that persists and queries the `Trades` to and from a database. Each trade, which is defined as a `Trade` POJO (refer to the code snippet defining a `Trade` shown earlier), will be persisted in the database representing a unique row (assuming the `id` is generated uniquely by our application) in the `TRADES` table.

There is nothing special about the persistence class from Hibernate's perspective. As the name suggests, they are plain old Java objects (or annotated Java objects) that Hibernate knows exactly how to handle.

The only bit that we have to discuss is the *identity* of the object. Hibernate mandates that every persistent object have a unique identifier. In the `Trade` class shown earlier, the `tradeId` variable forms a unique `Trade` object. It is the primary key of the table and hence persisted in the `TRADE_ID` column of our `TRADES` table. We must tell Hibernate about identifiers via our mapping definitions.

We can set the identifiers with some piece of code in our application or extract them from the database using, for example, a sequence number. We are going to learn about identifiers and how to generate them.

Using Annotations

Note that, conventionally, the mapping of the persistent classes to the database table is done outside of the code, via a mapping file (usually an XML file).

There is another way to do this. Java 5 introduced *annotations* to the language, which were very quickly adopted by many frameworks, including Hibernate. Annotations include metadata about a class that is added to the class at the source code level. They do not alter or affect how the actual source code works though.

 We will walk through Hibernate annotations in Chapter 3. For a brief introduction, however, we'll explore an example with annotations next.

Here's our modified `Trade` class, with mappings declared with annotations at the class and variable levels:

```
@Entity
@Table(name="TRADES")
public class Trade implements Serializable {
  @Id
  private long tradeId = -1;
  private double quantity = 0;
  private String security = null;
  // getters and setters
    ...
}
```

Each persistent object is tagged (at a class level) with an `@Entity` annotation. The `@Table` annotation declares our database table where these entities will be stored. Ideally, we should not have to provide the `@Table` annotation if the name of the class and the table name are the same (in our example, the class is `Trade`, whereas the table name is TRADES). The `@Id` annotation indicates that the variable is the unique identifier of the object instance (in other words, a primary key).

 As we are modifying the POJO to fit in the annotations, is it really a "plain" Java object anymore? There are arguments on both sides. In this book, I'll call them *annotated Java objects*!

Hibernate uses the Java Persistence API (JPA) annotations. JPA is the standard specification dictating the persistence of Java objects. So the preceding annotations are imported from the `javax.persistence` package.

We will be working with both (annotations and XML file) in this book, so tune in for the next few chapters to digest the details.

Once we have defined our persistent classes, the next step is to work on the configuration and mapping.

Configuration

In order to connect to a database, the Hibernate framework needs to know information about the database, such as its URL, credentials, and dialects. During the runtime of our application, this configuration is read by the framework to establish a connection to the database.

Hibernate database configuration is usually a one-off process. We saw in the previous chapter that the configuration is provided either via a properties file (*hibernate.properties*) or an XML file (*hibernate.cfg.xml*). However, we can use different filenames according to our preferences, in which case we need to tell Hibernate explicitly to load that file. The Hibernate runtime sweeps through the classpath for the default files to load them straightaway, if no other filename is specified.

Using a Properties File

The connection properties are provided as name/value pairs in the *hibernate.properties* file, as shown here:

```
#MySQL Properties
hibernate.connection.driver_class = com.mysql.jdbc.Driver
hibernate.connection.url = jdbc:mysql://localhost:3306/JH
hibernate.connection.username = myuser
hibernate.connection.password = mypassword
hibernate.dialect = org.hibernate.dialect.MySQL5Dialect
```

The preceding properties point to a MySQL database. We need to change the appropriate properties such as `driver_class`, `url`, and others when working with different databases. For example, the following snippet shows the connection details for Derby (an in-memory Java database, also called JavaDB):

```
#Derby Properties
hibernate.connection.driver_class = org.apache.derby.jdbc.EmbeddedDriver
hibernate.connection.url = jdbc:derby:memory:JH;create=true
hibernate.connection.username = myuser
hibernate.connection.password = mypassword
hibernate.dialect = org.hibernate.dialect.DerbyDialect
```

Make sure the vendor's driver classes are available in the classpath of the application. We can add them as dependencies in the *pom.xml* file if the project is a Maven-based module.

 The project associated with this book is a Maven-based project. Refer to "Setting Up Hibernate" on page 14 for details on how to set up the project.

Using the XML File

The alternative to using a properties file is declaring the metadata in an XML file as follows:

```xml
<?xml version="1.0" encoding="utf-8"?>
<hibernate-configuration>
  <session-factory>
    <property name="connection.url">jdbc:derby:memory:JH;create=true</property>
    <property name="connection.driver_class">
    org.apache.derby.jdbc.EmbeddedDriver</property>
    <property name="connection.username">jhuser</property>
    <property name="dialect">org.hibernate.dialect.DerbyDialect</property>
  </session-factory>
</hibernate-configuration>
```

As you may have noticed, the properties are used to create a `SessionFactory` object and hence declared under the `session-factory` tag. Also, the `hibernate.*` prefix is dropped here as opposed to the properties defined in the *hibernate.properties* file.

Configuration Properties

Now that you know how to wire in the properties to a Hibernate runtime, let's see what other properties we can use. Table 2-1 provides some important properties that you can configure.

Table 2-1. Configuration properties

Property	Values	Notes
hibernate.show_sql	true/false	If true, all the SQL statements are printed out
hibernate.jdbc.fetch_size	>=0	Set the JDBC fetch size
hibernate.jdbc.batch_size	>=	Used to batch the statements
hibernate.hbm2ddl.auto	validate/update/ create/create-drop	Schema options
hibernate.connection.pool_size	>=1	Connection pool size

Now that we have been given a choice of configurations (both the properties file and an XML file), you might be wondering which one to use. There is no hard-and-fast rule; you can use both of them if you wish. In fact, Hibernate's runtime does not complain if both of them are available to the application, but it simply ignores the properties file. So, any properties in the XML file take precedence over those in the properties file.

Programmatic Configuration

Both methods just discussed (properties and XML file) are declarative modes. Hibernate also supports programmatic configuration. In this case, you can use the appropriate classes to be instantiated with the `Configuration` class. This is shown in the following snippet:

```
Configuration cfg = new Configuration()
    .setProperty("hibernate.dialect", "org.hibernate.dialect.DerbyDialect")
    .setProperty("hibernate.connection.username", user);
    .setProperty("hibernate.connection.password", password);
    .setProperty("hibernate.connection.url", "jdbc:derby:memory:JH;create=true")
    .setProperty("hibernate.order_updates", "true");
```

Alternatively, you can pass the parameters as standard VM (virtual machine) arguments:

```
-Dhibernate.connection.url=jdbc:derby:memory:JH;create=true
-Dhibernate.username=mk
```

Mapping

The next thing we should think about is what kind of objects will be persisted by our application. We should also think about how object fields are mapped to the table columns and who controls what fields will be persisted.

By reading mapping XML files, Hibernate will transform object data to a row-column relational equivalent, which we discuss in the following sections.

Mapping is metadata that Hibernate digests to produce an object-to-relational data transformational plan. This plan lets us use object-oriented persistence in our Java applications with a relational database. As discussed earlier, we can use simple XML files or annotations to declare our metadata mapping.

XML Mapping Files

We will declare each domain POJO using the metadata in an XML file with an extension of *.hbm.xml*. This file should be made available in the classpath so Hibernate can bootstrap the mapping definitions.

For example, the `Trade` object mapping should be defined in the *Trade.hbm.xml* file, `Movie` in *Movie.hbm.xml*, and so on. It's not mandatory to declare one mapping file for one object; in fact, we can define the entire model in one single mapping file. That said, I would advise that you use one individual mapping for each persistent object, because this makes your mapping definitions and code easier to maintain, especially as your domain model becomes more complex.

So, the *Trade.hbm.xml* mapping definition file is as follows:

```
<hibernate-mapping>
  <class name="com.madhusudhan.jh.domain.Trade" table="TRADES">
    <id name="tradeId" column="TRADE_ID">
      <generator class="assigned"/>
    </id>
```

```
        <property name="quantity" column="QUANTITY"/>
        <property name="security" column="SECURITY"/>
    </class>
</hibernate-mapping>
```

There are a few things to take away from this file before we move on.

The class versus table mapping is done via a class tag, as highlighted in the preceding snippet. The class declaration simply says that our Trade object will be persisted to the TRADES table. You can see that a table attribute is defined too; this would indicate where the objects are saved.

In addition to declaring the mapping from the class to a table, we need to tell Hibernate which object properties should be persisted.

The first (and most important) of the list of persistent properties is the identifier (or primary key) of the object. The tradeId is mapped to the primary key of the table TRADE_ID via the id tag. The name of the id tag corresponds to the variable tradeId we defined on the Trade class. Hibernate calls the getTradeId and setTradeId accordingly to set or get the TRADE_ID variable.

The field to which our Trade object will be persisted is defined by the property tag. In the preceding example, the quantity field on the Trade object will be stored in the QUANTITY column as defined by the column tag, and the security value is mapped to the SECURITY column.

There is a simpler way to create a mapping. If the name of the column matches the variable name of the object, we can omit the declaration of the column property. Thus, we can modify the previous example and omit the column tags for quantity and security (as the variable names match the column names):

```
<hibernate-mapping>
    <class name="com.madhusudhan.jh.domain.Trade" table="TRADES">
        ...
        <property name="quantity"/>
        <property name="security"/>
    </class>
</hibernate-mapping>
```

In the preceding snippet, we omitted mentioning the data types of our attributes. How does Hibernate knows that quantity is a double type or security is a String type? Well, ideally we should declare the types too, using the type tag, as shown here:

```
<hibernate-mapping>
    <class name="com.madhusudhan.jh.domain.Trade" table="TRADES">
        ...
        <property name="quantity" type="double"/>
        <property name="security" type="string"/>
    </class>
</hibernate-mapping>
```

We can omit these types and let Hibernate work out the variable types (by using Java reflection) or we can explicitly declare them.

My personal preference is to declare them explicitly to reduce the startup, as Hibernate will not waste time finding out the types by using Java reflection.

While the mapping example just shown is the simplest one, we can do more by adding associations, relationships, queries, and other Hibernate elements. We will revisit this topic again in coming chapters.

So, now we have two sets of files: *hibernate.cfg.xml* (or *hibernate.properties*) and *Trade.hbm.xml* (our domain mapping file). We need to reference the mapping file in the configuration file so Hibernate can pick up the mappings during its bootstrap along with its usual database configuration.

Here's a snippet from the configuration file, showing how to reference mapping file(s):

```
<hibernate-configuration>
  <session-factory>
    <property name="connection.url">
      jdbc:derby:memory:JH;create=true
    </property>
    ...
    <mapping resource="Movie.hbm.xml" />
    <mapping resource="Trade.hbm.xml" />
  </session-factory>
</hibernate-configuration>
```

Identifier Generation Strategies

Each object must be persisted to a database with a unique identifier. We can use different strategies for generating these identifiers automatically. Hibernate provides a rich set of such strategies, which we will see in this section.

As you have seen in earlier examples, we define a generator class for setting up an id element as follows:

```
<hibernate-mapping>
  <class name="com.madhusudhan.jh.domain.Movie" table="MOVIES">
    <id name="id" column="MOVIE_ID">
      <generator class="assigned"/>
    </id>
    ...
  </class>
</hibernate-mapping>
```

The generator is the key element that lets Hibernate know our choice of identifier generation strategy. The class attribute on the generator defines the actual strategy we are going to use. For example, in the preceding snippet, we are using *assigned strategy*, meaning our code is expected to set a unique identifier on each of the persistent objects.

The "assigned" is a shortcut name for the org.hibernate.id.Assigned class. Instead of requiring us to provide the fully qualified name of the generator class, Hibernate lets us use a short version for our convenience. For example, the "sequence" name corresponds to org.hibernate.id.SequenceGenerator, "identity" corresponds to org.hibernate.id.IdentityGenerator, and so on. All these classes implement a common interface, org.hibernate.id.IdentifierGenerator.

Hibernate offers quite a few generators out of the box—for example, identity, sequence, native, and assigned. Should you have a specific requirement of your own primary key generation strategy, you can create a custom strategy by implementing the Identifier Generator interface and providing the custom logic.

We can specify required arguments to these generators using param elements. For example, when using sequence strategy, we need to let Hibernate know what our sequencer table is:

```
<id name="id" column="MOVIE_ID">
  <generator class="sequence">
        <param name="sequence">MOVIE_SEQUENCE</param>
  </generator>
</id>
```

I would recommend that you refer to Hibernate's reference documentation to run through the various strategies Hibernate provides.

Session APIs

Hibernate comes with a rich set of APIs for object persistence and retrieval. While looking at the entire API set is outside the scope of this book, we'll discuss the most important and fundamental Session APIs, which are necessary for understanding Hibernate concepts.

We had a primer on Hibernate's most basic APIs earlier in the chapter. The Session Factory, represented by the org.hibernate.SessionFactory class, is a factory class for churning out our Session instances. It is a thread-safe object and hence can be shared across various classes without our having to worry about the data being corrupted. We supply the mapping information to this class upon creation, so it contains all the mapping data in a compiled form.

If you remember correctly, we created this factory by providing the configuration data. For example:

```
private SessionFactory getSessionFactory() {
  Configuration config = new Configuration().configure("hibernate.cfg.xml");
  ServiceRegistry registry =
    new  ServiceRegistryBuilder()
          .applySettings(config.getProperties())
```

```
        .buildServiceRegistry();
    return config.buildSessionFactory(registry);
}
```

Note that we are using Hibernate's newly introduced (in 4.x) service registry classes to create the configuration.

The SessionFactory also maintains a second level of cache, which is available globally across all other components in the application. Global cache is used if multiple applications require the same data that's been loaded from the database. This will speed up the application's request times.

While SessionFactory holds the access keys to the doors of a database, the Session itself is the key to interact with and access the database. Session is a single-threaded object and therefore should not be shared across various components. It represents a single unit of work. We use factory.getCurrentSession() to fetch a session from the factory. Once we have the session object, we can perform our database operations in a transaction. The Session and Transaction go hand in hand. The usual life cycle of the session and a transaction is demonstrated in the following snippet:

```
// Get a current session
Session session = factory.getCurrentSession();
// Create a transaction and start it
Transaction tx = session.getTransaction();
tx.begin();
// Do your database operations with the session
// Once done, commit the transaction and session
tx.commit();
```

Note that the first level of cache is maintained in the session; (i.e., all the objects that were fetched or accessed will be held in the session until the session is closed). We should not use the session per individual operations. Ideally, all the related database operations should be grouped under one transaction.

Transactions

One of the fundamental pieces in performing actions on business data is to work with transactions. In simple terms, transactions keep our work segregated from others, and synchronize with the durable storage to avoid incorrect data being read or written. There are four fundamental properties that database transactions revolve around: atomicity, consistency, isolation, and durability, which are collectively known as ACID properties. Understanding transactions will help you design great software.

Take the example of booking a train ticket from London to Paris on EuroStar. When you pay for your ticket, you want the ticket to be confirmed and your seat allocated all in one go. Should there be a hiccup in the booking process, you wouldn't want to have spent your money and have no booking! So either everything should go in an orderly fashion, succeeding at each step, or the entire process should abort if any step fails in processing this order. This sequence of steps is encompassed in a *transaction*.

Typically, there are two modes of fetching transactions: a container can create and manage your work in its transaction, or we can create our own transaction. Obviously, in the former case, we don't have to worry about transaction semantics such as committing and rolling back the transactions; these are all taken care of by the container.

In a standalone JVM, we need to work with the transaction exclusively. The following snippet persists the Course object to the durable storage space:

```
private void persist() {
  Transaction tx = null;
  try {
    // Create a Transaction instance
      tx = session.beginTransaction();

      // Start our task of creating
      // and persisting the course instance
    Course course = createCourse();
    session.save(course);

    // Hooray, mission accomplished!
    tx.commit();
  } catch (HibernateException he) {
  // Houston, we have a problem!
  // Mission aborted!
      if(tx!=null)
        tx.rollback();
    throw he;
      }finally{
    // We must close the transaction
    session.close();
  }
}
```

We initiate a transaction by invoking the session.beginTrasaction method, which creates a new Transaction object and returns the reference to us. It gets associated with the session and is open until that transaction is committed or rolled back.

We perform the required work in a transaction, then issue a commit on this transaction. At this stage, the entities are persisted to the database. While persisting, if for whatever reason there are any errors, the Hibernate runtime will catch and throw a HibernateEx ception (which is an unchecked RuntimeException). We then have to catch the exception and roll back the transaction. We may throw additional exceptions back to the client for information or debugging purposes.

Summary

In this chapter, we tried to understand the fundamental building blocks of Hibernate. We discussed the object-relational paradigm mismatch and ORM tools, such as the Hibernate framework, in solving this mismatch. We then delved into the details of configuring Hibernate, mapping the classes to the database tables, and the design of persistent entities.

CHAPTER 3

Annotations

Annotations were introduced in Java 5, and since then most of the toolkits have started using them heavily. Annotations are decorators applied at the class and variable level that define the metadata about the class itself. Hibernate embraced annotations closely and integrated them with the core as first-class citizens. As they are a necessary tool in developing sophisticated ORM mappings, we will be learning about them in detail in this chapter. We'll also discuss the pros and cons of using annotations versus traditional XML files toward the end of the chapter.

In earlier chapters, we worked with the mapping of persistent classes using XML files. Using XML files for our configuration and mapping has both advantages and disadvantages. For one thing, they are quite simple and easily readable, but they are also quite verbose and unfortunately do not impose type safety. Annotations, on the other hand, are quite concise and enable compile-type checks straightaway. They are metadata decorations applied directly on the class, therefore enabling the entities to be managed effectively. We discussed annotations briefly earlier, but now we'll revisit and learn about them in detail.

Working Through an Example

As always, beginning with a simple example will help you on your path of learning annotations. Let's start with a simple persistent class, `Employee`, defined without annotations (pure POJO) here:

```
public class Employee {
  private int id =0;
  private String name = null;
  ...
}
```

To make this class persistent using annotations, we first define it as an `Entity`. We do so by annotating the class with the `@Entity` annotation. Simple, eh?

```
@Entity
public class Employee {
  private int id =0;
  private String name = null;
  ...
}
```

Now that we have a persistent entity, our next step is to define an identifier. Remember, all persistent entities must have their identifiers defined; otherwise, Hibernate will moan and groan. So, we use the `@Id` annotation to indicate the object's identifier to the framework. In our `Employee` class, our primary key is declared as an `id` variable, so we decorate the `id` with the relevant annotation:

```
@Entity
public class Employee {
  @Id
  private int id =0;
  private String name = null;
  public int getId() {
    return id;
  }
  ...
}
```

When we annotate the `id` variable with the `@Id` annotation, as in the preceding example, Hibernate maps a field called `ID` from our `EMPLOYEE` table to the `id` variable on the `Employee` class.

Did you notice that we've decorated the variable instead of a getter method? Well, we do have a choice: we can either use the annotation on a variable, in which case Hibernate uses field access, or we can use it on an accessor method, in which case Hibernate uses the accessor method to access the field. There is no hard-and-fast rule here; it's pretty much a personal preference. I usually prefer annotating variable definitions, so that's what I use for this book's examples.

One more thing to note: most databases will not allow us to create a field called `ID`, as it is a reserved keyword. In such circumstances, we usually change the field name—for example, `EMPLOYEE_ID` in the preceding `EMPLOYEE` table's case. As the object field and the column name do not match, we need to set the column name explicitly using an additional annotation, `@Column`, as shown here:

```
@Entity
public class Employee {
  @Id
  @Column(name="EMPLOYEE_ID")
  private int id =0;
  ...
```

Before we delve into `Entity` and `Id` annotation options, let's first see how the example is working.

We must let the Hibernate configuration know about our annotated classes. You can do this in two ways: declaratively in your mapping file or programatically in your class.

In your *hibernate.cfg.xml* file, use the mapping element to declare your class. Here's how we do it via the mapping file:

```
<hibernate-configuration>
    ...
    <mapping class="com.madhusudhan.jh.annotations.Employee"/>
</hibernate-configuration>
```

Alternatively, use the `addAnnotatedClass` method if you prefer associating the annotation in your program:

```
Configuration config = new Configuration()
 .configure("annotations/hibernate.cfg.xml");
 .addAnnotatedClass(Employee.class)
 .addAnnotatedClass(Director.class);
...
```

Notice the chaining of the methods on the `Configuration` class. This is a convenient way of including additional methods in the class.

Run your test class, and it should persist your `Employee` object without any hiccups!

Digging into Details

Now that we have seen a simple example in action, it's time to get into the meat of annotations.

In our `Employee` example, the name of the table is the same as that of the class (`EMPLOYEE` and `Employee`, respectively). Thus, we did not mention the table name when declaring the `@Entity` annotation. Let's suppose our table name is `TBL_EMPLOYEE`; then we need to let Hibernate know that by adding an `@Table` annotation too:

```
@Entity
@Table(name = "TBL_EMPLOYEE")
public class Employee {
  ...
}
```

Similarly, as we have already seen in the case of `id`, if your variable doesn't match the column name, you must specify the column name using the `@Column` annotation:

```
@Entity
@Table(name = "TBL_EMPLOYEE")
public class Employee {
  ...
```

```
@Column(name="EMPLOYEE_NAME")
private int name =0;
}
```

We can also set a few more options for each column using the @Column attributes. For example, if the column accepts non-null data, we fulfill this option by setting nullable=false. Or we specify unique=true if the column should be generated with a unique constraint. These attributes are shown in the following snippet:

```
@Entity
@Table(name = "TBL_EMPLOYEE")
public class Employee {
  @Id
  @Column(name="EMPLOYEE_ID", nullable = false, unique = true)
  private int empoyeeId = 0;
  ...
```

We can set the identifier of each object by employing various strategies. We'll see this in the next section.

ID Generation Strategies

Hibernate provides various identifier generation strategies using annotations, similar to what we have seen in XML mappings. In the previous snippet, the ID generation strategy was not set, meaning it is by default employing an AUTO strategy. When the strategy is AUTO, Hibernate relies on our database to generate primary keys. For example, if we have defined a primary key with the AUTO_INCREMENT option in MySQL, Hibernate uses that option accordingly.

We can set up different strategies depending on our requirements. All we need to do is add @GeneratedValue annotation to the id variable. This annotation accepts two attributes: strategy and generator. The strategy attribute indicates the type of identifier generation that we would like to use, while generator defines the methods to generate the identifiers.

The following code snippet uses the IDENTITY strategy for its ID generation:

```
@Entity(name = "TBL_EMPLOYEE")
public class Employee {
  @Id
  @Column(name="ID")
  @GeneratedValue(strategy = GenerationType.IDENTITY)
  private int employeeId =0;
    ...
}
```

Notice that for the IDENTITY strategy, we have to provide the generator method, as this depends upon the identity function provided by the database. The identity function is supported by a few databases, including MySQL, Sybase, and DB2.

The strategy should be the GeneratorType value, as described in the following:

GeneratorType.AUTO

This is the default strategy and is portable across different databases. Hibernate chooses the appropriate ID based on the database.

GeneratorType.IDENTITY

This setting is based on the identity provided by some databases; it is the responsibility of the database to provide a unique identifier.

GeneratorType.SEQUENCE

Some databases provide a mechanism of sequenced numbers, so this setting will let Hibernate use the sequence number.

GeneratorType.TABLE

Sometimes the primary keys have been created from a unique column in another table. In this case, use the TABLE generator.

For employing a sequence strategy, you must define both the strategy and the sequence generator:

```
public class Employee {
  @Id
  @Column(name="EMPLOYEE_ID")
  @GeneratedValue (strategy= GenerationType.SEQUENCE, generator="empSeqGen")
  @SequenceGenerator(name = "empSeqGen", sequenceName = "EMP_SEQ_GEN")
  private int employeeId =0;
  ...
}
```

The strategy is defined as a SEQUENCE, and accordingly the generator is given a reference to a sequence generator, empSeqGen, which refers to a sequence object in the database. Using the @SequenceGenerator, we reference EMP_SEQ_GEN, which is a sequence object created in the database.

As with sequences, we can use an @TableGenerator strategy if we have a database table that provides our primary keys. The following snippet demonstrates this:

```
public class Employee {
  @Id
  @Column(name="ID")
  @GeneratedValue (strategy= GenerationType.TABLE, generator="empTableGen")
  @TableGenerator(name = "empTableGen", table = "EMP_ID_TABLE")
  private int empoyeeId =0;
  ...
}
```

Composite Identifiers

We don't always have a single column (surrogate key) as our primary key identifying the unique row. Sometimes we have a combination of columns providing a *business* key, commonly called a *composite* or *compound key*. In this case, we need to use a different mechanism for setting the appropriate object identifier.

There are three ways of setting the composite-id identifiers, which we will see in the next sections.

Using Primary Key Class and @Id

In this method, we create a separate class representing the business key. We annotate this class with @Embeddable, making it a composite-id class.

In the following example, the CoursePK consists of two variables, tutor and title. The combination of these two attributes makes a composite key for Course class.

```
@Embeddable
public class CoursePK implements Serializable{
  private String tutor = null;
  private String title = null;
  // Default constructor
  public CoursePK() {
  }
  ...
}
```

Notice that the class has been decorated with the @Embeddable annotation.

Make sure the class implements the java.io.Serializable interface with a default constructor. Also, it must have the hashCode and equals methods implemented; they will help Hibernate distinguish uniqueness.

The next step is to *embed* this class on our persistent class's id variable. We do this by using our simple @Id annotation:

```
@Entity
@Table(name="COURSE_ANNOTATION")
public class Course {
  @Id
  private CoursePK id = null;
  private int totalStudents = 0;
  private int registeredStudents = 0;

  public CoursePK getId() {
    return id;
  }
  public void setId(CoursePK id) {
    this.id = id;
```

```
    }
    ...
}
```

The Course persistent POJO has three variables: id, totalStudents, and registered Students. As we know, the id is a CoursePK type—a composite class with two variables, tutor and title—making up the primary class for our Course object.

Run a test case and see how the composite key has been formed on the table:

```
private void persist() {
    ...
    Course course = new Course();
    CoursePK coursePk = new CoursePK();
    coursePk.setTitle("Computer Science");
    coursePk.setTutor("Prof. Harry Barry");

    course.setId(coursePk);
    course.setTotalStudents(20);
    course.setRegisteredStudents(12);
    session.save(course);
    ...
}
```

Execute the SELECT statement on the table to check the result, as shown in Table 3-1.

Table 3-1. Using @Id table results

TITLE	TUTOR	REGISTERED_STUDENTS	TOTAL_STUDENTS
Computer Science	Prof. Harry Barry	12	20

Now, let's see the second method of creating composite identifiers.

Using Primary Key Class and @EmbeddedId

In this case, we annotate the identifier of the Course object with @EmbeddedId (instead of annotating with @Id as we did in our earlier case). At the same time, we create an inner class, @CoursePK, annotating with @Embeddable:

```
@Entity
@Table(name = "COURSE_ANNOTATION_V2")
public class Course2 {
  @EmbeddedId
  private CoursePK2 id = null;
  private int totalStudents = 0;
  private int registeredStudents = 0;

  public Course2(String title, String tutor) {
    id = new CoursePK2();
    id.setTitle(title);
    id.setTutor(tutor);
  }
```

```
    . . .
}
```

The `id` field is annotated with `@EmbeddedId` in the preceding class. Notice that the constructor is doing the job of creating and populating the composite primary key. You can do this outside of the constructor too, if you wish.

However, we do not have to annotate `@Embeddable` on the primary key class, as we did in the first method. See the plain definition (i.e., no annotations) of the primary key class `CoursePK2` class here:

```
public class CoursePK2 implements Serializable {
    private String tutor = null;
    private String title = null;
    // Default constructor
    public CoursePK2() { }
    // Implement hashCode and equals methods
    @Override
    public int hashCode() { ... }
    @Override
    public boolean equals(Object obj) { ... }
```

This is a simple class that adheres to the primary composite class rules—having a default constructor, and the `hashCode` and `equals` method implementations.

Create a test client to persist the object:

```
private void persist() {
    Course2 course = new Course2("Financial Risk Management", "Harry Barry");
    course.setTotalStudents(20);
    course.setRegisteredStudents(12);
    session.save(course);
    . . .
}
```

We instantiate the `Course2` object with `title` and `tutor`, which internally creates the composite key by setting these values on the `CoursePK2` object.

When you run the client, the table will be populated with the composite key and the class information, just as you would expect. The `SELECT` statement will get the same results as in the first case.

Now let's discuss the third way of implementing the composite key strategy.

Using @IdClass

In this method, we create a composite class (primary key) with all the required primary key attributes. However, we do not annotate this class, so it remains a plain Java class. Here's the definition:

```
public class CoursePK3 implements Serializable {
  private String tutor = null;
  private String title = null;
  public CoursePK3() {}
  ...
}
```

Now we need to declare the main entity with the additional class-level annotation @IdClass. This refers to our composite primary key class.

When it comes to the main entity class, there is a disadvantage of following this path. We need to duplicate the composite key identifiers (tutor and title) on our main class too in this method. They must be decorated with @Id.

See the class definition of our main entity class here:

```
@IdClass(value = CoursePK3.class)
@Entity
@Table(name = "COURSE_ANNOTATION_V3")
public class Course3 {

  // We must duplicate the identifiers
  // defined in our primary class here too
  @Id
  private String title = null;
  @Id
  private String tutor = null;
  ...
}
```

Using the @IdClass method for defining the composite key is not a standard practice and is best avoided. I suggest you pick either of the first two methods instead.

POJOs Versus AJOs

When working with annotations, we *decorate* the source classes with metadata, thus potentially losing the "plain" nature of these POJOs in the bargain. So, some people argue that they are not POJOs anymore. On the other hand, annotations are simply Java's markup lingo, so they may still fall under the category of POJOs. To put the argument to rest, instead of calling them POJOs, we will call them *annotated Java objects (AJOs)*.

Summary

In this chapter, we learned about annotations in general and how Hibernate supports them. We began by walking through an example and identifying various annotations such as @Entity, @Id, @Table, @Column, and others. We have also learned about the identifier generation strategies, using the appropriate annotations.

Annotations do not stop here; there are many other annotations used across Hibernate for various purposes. Anything that we can do using XML mappings, we should be able to do using annotations. As we continue our journey learning Hibernate in this book, we will learn how to use annotations alongside the XML mappings.

CHAPTER 4

Persisting Collections

Working with data structures, formally known as *Java collections*, is inevitable for any Java developer. In this chapter, we will learn about Hibernate's support for persisting and retrieving collections. We will look in detail at how we can persist the standard Java collections using the Hibernate framework.

As a Java developer, at some point in your programming life, you have probably worked with Java collections. Java collections are the most common data structures in Java, with various algorithm features.

We will, at some point, encounter persistent objects with collections as their values. Persisting simple values from Hibernate's view is different from persisting collection elements such as `java.util.List` or `java.util.Map` structures. We need to follow certain mapping procedures and processes to let Hibernate know our intentions.

The familiar Java collections—such as `List`, `Set`, `Array`, and `Map`—are all supported by Hibernate. In fact, it goes one step further and creates a couple of other collections, such as `bag` and `idbag`. Let's look at them one by one.

Designing to Interfaces

Java provides collection interfaces such as `java.util.Collection` (which is the parent to all the collection interfaces except the map interface), `java.util.List` (the interface for list data structures), `java.util.Set` (for set data structures), `java.util.Map` (for key/value map data structures), and more.

The `List` implementation is intended to hold ordered lists of elements. We use concrete implementations, such as `ArrayList` or `LinkedList`, but the point here is that we must design to the `List` interface in our Hibernate application rather than to its concrete implementation.

Always use interfaces when you are defining your collection variables. Hibernate does not like it when we use concrete classes as the variable types:

```
ArrayList<String> actors = new ArrayList<String>();
```

Instead, we should define the types using interfaces, like so:

```
List<String> actors = new ArrayList<String>();
```

The reason is that behind the scenes, Hibernate uses its own implementation of List!

Next we'll explore the mechanics of persisting one of the most widely used collection structures—lists!

Persisting Lists

Lists are simple and easy data structures to hold items in an orderly manner. They can also keep track of an element's position, using indexes. We can insert an element anywhere in the list, and retrieve the element using its index.

For example, let's say we have persisted a list of manufacturers (Toyota, BMW, Mercedes, etc.) via our Java program. We should expect to retrieve the car data from the table in the same order in which it was inserted. So, if we run a query list.get(n), we should get back the *nth* element without fail.

To satisfy this requirement, Hibernate maintains another table with the cars' indexes. So, when it fetches the cars from the main table, it also fetches the indexed order of these items from the additional table (called, say, CAR_LIST). It will then associate and map these items together to find out the order, and accordingly feed the client with the ordered responses.

But enough theory. How can we persist our cars list using Hibernate? To get a better understanding, let's see an example.

List Example: Car Showroom

Consider a simple case of a car showroom. A showroom consists of dozens of cars for customers to view and possibly purchase. We can represent this with a simple model.

Every showroom will have a variety of cars to sell. Some cars may be brand new, while others are secondhand. We model these cars as java.util.List, as shown here in Showroom's implementation (along with the Car definition):

```
// Showroom class
public class Showroom {
  private int id = 0;
  private String manager = null;
```

```
  private String location = null;
  private List<Car> cars = null;
  ...
  // Setters and getters
}

// Car class
public class Car {
  private int id;
  private String name = null;
  private String color = null;
  ...
  // Setters and getters
}
```

The Showroom and Car classes are very simple POJOs. The only notable point is the declaration of a one-to-many association of Showroom with cars—that is, one showroom consists of many cars.

Once the POJOs are ready, we add the mapping definitions:

```
<hibernate-mapping package="com.madhusudhan.jh.collections.list">

  <!-- Showroom class mapping definition -->

  <class name="Showroom" table="SHOWROOM_LIST">
    <id column="SHOWROOM_ID" name="id">
      <generator class="native"/>
    </id>
    ...
    <list name="cars" cascade="all" table="CARS_LIST">
      <key column="SHOWROOM_ID"/>
      <index column="CAR_INDEX"/>
      <one-to-many class="Car"/>
    </list>
  </class>

  <!-- Car class mapping definition -->

  <class name="Car" table="CARS_LIST">
    <id column="CAR_ID" name="id">
      <generator class="native"/>
    </id>
    <property column="NAME" name="name"/>
    <property column="COLOR" name="color"/>
  </class>
</hibernate-mapping>
```

Notice the use of the list element in the preceding snippet. This element defines the mapping of the cars declared in the Showroom object to the table.

The main table, SHOWROOM_LIST, will be created and populated as expected, so there are no surprises there. However, CARS_LIST is an additional table that gets created in the process. In addition to the CAR_ID, NAME, and COLOR properties present in the CARS_LIST table, which are directly declared on the object itself, Hibernate creates two other columns. One of them is a foreign key, SHOWROOM_ID, while the other is the CAR_INDEX column to hold the list indexes. CAR_INDEX is populated with each list element's position, and is used later to reconstruct the list elements in their original positions.

When retrieving the cars, at runtime, Hibernate reorders the records according to the index held in CAR_INDEX. Let's run the test client to check out how this works in practice.

Test Client for List Persistence

Fire up a small test client to test the list persistence functionality, as shown here:

```
private void persistLists() {
  // Create showroom object
  Showroom showroom = new Showroom();
  showroom.setLocation("East Croydon, Greater London");
  showroom.setManager("Barry Larry");

  // Create list of cars
  List<Car> cars = new ArrayList<Car>();
  cars.add(new Car("Toyota", "Racing Green"));
  cars.add(new Car("Toyota", "Racing Green"));
  cars.add(new Car("Nissan", "White"));
  cars.add(new Car("BMW", "Black"));
  cars.add(new Car("Mercedes", "Silver"));

  ...
  // Associate cars to the showroom
  showroom.setCars(cars);

  // Save the showroom
  session.save(showroom);
}
```

The test client is self-explanatory. Notice that I'm adding an extra Toyota to the list! When you run the test to retrieve the results, the following output is printed to the console (check out the duplicate Toyota cars too in the output!):

```
Showroom{id=6, manager=Barry Larry, location=East Croydon, Greater London, cars=[
Car{id=15, name=Toyota, color=Racing Green},
Car{id=16, name=Toyota, color=Racing Green},
Car{id=17, name=Nissan, color=White},
Car{id=18, name=BMW, color=Black},
Car{id=19, name=Mercedes, color=Silver}]]
```

As you can see, Hibernate honors the insertion order of the cars in the list.

Persisting Sets

`java.util.Set` represents an unordered data structure where duplicates are not allowed. Using sets is straightforward just like lists. We'll revisit the showroom cars example from the previous example to demonstrate how sets are used with Hibernate.

In our modified example, the collection of cars that belong to a showroom is modeled as `java.util.Set`; thus we define the `cars` variable as the `Set` type. We use `HashSet` as our concrete implementation of the `Set` interface.

The `Showroom` class is shown here:

```java
public class Showroom {
  private int id = 0;
  private String manager = null;
  private String location = null;

  // Cars are represented as set
  private Set<Car> cars = null;

  // Getters and setters
  ...
```

The notable change is the use of the `Set` collection instead of `List`. Once you finish modifying the `Showroom` class, the mapping of `Set` is done via the `set` tag, as demonstrated in the following snippet:

```xml
<hibernate-mapping package="com.madhusudhan.jh.collections.set">
  <!- The showroom class. Note the mapping of cars -->
  <class name="Showroom" table="SHOWROOM_SET">
    <id column="SHOWROOM_ID" name="id">
      <generator class="native"/>
    </id>
    ...
    <set name="cars" table="CARS_SET" cascade="all">
      <key column="SHOWROOM_ID"/>
      <one-to-many class="Car"/>
    </set>
  </class>

  <!-- The car mapping definition - very simple -->
  <class name="Car" table="CARS_SET">
    <id column="CAR_ID" name="id">
      <generator class="native"/>
    </id>
    <property column="NAME" name="name"/>
    <property column="COLOR" name="color"/>
  </class>
</hibernate-mapping>
```

A Showroom instance is mapped to SHOWROOM_SET table, whereas the cars variable representing the set collection is mapped to the CARS_SET table, as expected. The key element represents the presence of a foreign key in the CARS_SET table. Hibernate adds this foreign key to the CARS_SET table automatically. Hence, the CARS_SET table, which is created and managed by Hibernate, will have the additional foreign key SHOW ROOM_ID, thus associating the two tables.

Create a test client as shown here:

```java
private void persistSets() {
    // Create and populate showroom
    Showroom showroom = new Showroom();
    showroom.setLocation("East Croydon, Greater London");
    showroom.setManager("Barry Larry");

    // Create and populate cars set
    Set<Car> cars = new HashSet<Car>();

    cars.add(new Car("Toyota", "Racing Green"));
    cars.add(new Car("Nissan", "White"));
    cars.add(new Car("BMW", "Black"));
    cars.add(new Car("BMW", "Black"));

    // Associate cars to the showroom and persist it
    showroom.setCars(cars);
    session.save(showroom);
    ...
}
```

In the preceding example, we created a Showroom object to which we've added three new cars. We are using HashSet as our concrete implementation for our cars collection. Did you notice that we are trying to add another BMW to the set? The set would identify these two cars as identical based on equality matching and hence would throw away the duplicate one.

When working with sets, we need to satisfy an equality requirement: we must create equals and hashCode methods in the Car object. As we know, each individual item that's being added to the set must be unique. The equals and hashCode methods would help to satisfy this requirement. Make sure the equals and hashCode contracts are fulfilled correctly—for example, use the fields that will identify a car uniquely.

The retrieveSets test method would fetch the persisted set from the database, as shown in this listing:

```
Showroom{id=7, manager=Barry Larry, location=East Croydon, Greater London, cars=[
Car{id=27, name=Nissan, color=White},
Car{id=26, name=Mercedes, color=Silver},
Car{id=28, name=Toyota, color=Racing Green},
Car{id=29, name=BMW, color=Black}]}
...
```

Did you notice that the BMW isn't listed twice, although we added another to the set earlier? This demonstrates the set's "exclusion of duplicates" policy.

Persisting Maps

When you have a requirement to represent name/value pairs, your first choice should be Maps. The Map data structures are like dictionaries where you have a key (word) and related values (meanings). Maps are the de facto choice for key/value-paired data, such as bank accounts (value) of a single customer (key) or stock quotes for an issuer.

Continuing with our car showroom example, next we'll add the capability for the showroom to hold potential customers' reservations for test driving cars. We can best implement this functionality by employing a Map data structure, linking customers to car reservations:

```
public class Showroom {
  private int id = 0;
  private String manager = null;
  private String location = null;
  private Map<String, Car> cars = null;

  // getters & setters
  ...
```

Each car is reserved for a customer, and all the cars belong to the showroom. We can implement the customer-to-cars data type as a Map<String, Car> type.

The main meat is in the mapping, which is defined here:

```
<hibernate-mapping package="com.madhusudhan.jh.collections.map">
  <!-- Showroom mapping definition with cars variable
  mapped to CARS_MAP table using map tag -->

  <class name="Showroom" table="SHOWROOM_MAP">
    <id column="SHOWROOM_ID" name="id">
      <generator class="native"/>
    </id>
    <property column="MANAGER" name="manager"/>
    ...
    <map name="cars" cascade="all" table="CARS_MAP">
      <key column="SHOWROOM_ID"/>
      <map-key column="CUST_NAME" type="string" />
      <one-to-many class="Car"/>
    </map>
  </class>

  <!-- Simple Car class-table mapping -->
  <class name="Car" table="CARS_MAP">
    <id column="CAR_ID" name="id">
      <generator class="native"/>
```

```
        </id>
        <property name="name" column="CAR_NAME" />
        <property name="color" column="COLOR" />
    </class>
</hibernate-mapping>
```

As expected, the showroom's `cars` variable is represented by a `map` element referring to a table, CARS_MAP, in the mapping definition. The `map` element defines a foreign key (SHOWROOM_ID, in this case). The `map-key` attribute defines the key of the map—the customer, in our case. The car class mapping is a simple and straightforward one. Note that Hibernate would add a couple of more columns to the CARS_MAP table—SHOW ROOM_ID and CUST_NAME—in addition to the name and `color` columns.

Once the mapping is done, we need to demonstrate its workings using a test client as follows:

```
private void persistMaps() {
    Showroom showroom = new Showroom();
    showroom.setLocation("East Croydon, Greater London");
    showroom.setManager("Cherry Flurry");

    Map<String, Car> cars = new HashMap<String, Car>();
    cars.put("barry", new Car("Toyota", "Racing Green"));
    cars.put("larry", new Car("Nissan", "White"));
    cars.put("harry", new Car("BMW", "Black"));

    showroom.setCars(cars);
    ...
}
```

Here we create a map with a customer name and the cars to test drive. We then attach them to the showroom. As you can see in our `Map` data structure, we have a brand new car corresponding to a customer.

As expected, the following output would be printed to the console if we run the `retrie veMaps` method on the client:

```
Showroom{id=1, manager=Cherry Flurry, location=East Croydon, Greater London,
cars={barry=Car{id=1, name=Toyota, color=Racing Green},
harry=Car{id=2, name=BMW, color=Black},
larry=Car{id=3, name=Nissan, color=White},
fairy=Car{id=4, name=Mercedes, color=Pink}}}
...
```

The output shows all the cars in the showroom are reserved to customers for a test drive.

Persisting Arrays

Persisting arrays is similar to persisting lists, so we will only breeze through the mechanics and will not delve into too much detail here. The Showroom class now has a variable, cars, of the String array type, as listed here:

```
public class Showroom {
  private int id = 0;
  private String manager = null;
  private String location = null;
  // List of cars
  private String[] cars = null;
  ...
```

The mapping of the classes is defined here:

```
<hibernate-mapping package="com.madhusudhan.jh.collections.array">
  <class name="Showroom" table="SHOWROOM_ARRAY">
    <id column="SHOWROOM_ID" name="id">
      <generator class="native"/>
    </id>
    ...
    <array name="cars" cascade="all" table="CARS_ARRAY">
      <key column="SHOWROOM_ID"/>
      <index column="CAR_INDEX"/>
      <element column="CAR_NAME" type="string" not-null="true"/>
    </array>
  </class>
</hibernate-mapping>
```

The array tag defines the mapping between the cars variable and the CARS_ARRAY table. As expected, the CARS_ARRAY table will have a foreign key (SHOWROOM_ID, in this case). Hibernate also preserves the insertion order; hence, index tag must be defined with a name. element defines the actual values composing the array—in this case, the model name of each car.

The persistArrays method on our test class (shown next) would persist the relevant arrays in the database. We create the String[] of cars, passing in the model names, as shown in the following snippet:

```
private void persistArrays() {
  ...
  Showroom showroom = new Showroom();
  showroom.setLocation("East Croydon, Greater London");
  showroom.setManager("Barry Larry");

  // Create array of cars and
  // associate with the showroom
  String[] cars = new String[]{"Toyota","BMW","Citroen"};
  showroom.setCars(cars);
```

```
    // Normal saving of the showroom
    session.save(showroom);
    ...
  }
```

The `retrieveArrays` method on the test client would fetch the cars as expected:

```
Showroom{id=9, manager=Barry Larry, location=East Croydon, Greater London,
cars=[Toyota, BMW, Citroen]}
```

Persisting Bags and IdBags

If we wish to have an unordered collection and no indexing of the elements, Java doesn't have any data structure that supports that. The closest is `java.util.List`, but obviously it maintains both order and indexing. To satisfy this requirement, Hibernate created a special type of collection called *bags*.

Bags are the opposite of lists: they are unordered and nonindexed collections that allow duplicate elements. Bags are unique to Hibernate, and there is no equivalent collection in the Java space.

Implementing bags is very simple; we don't notice any difference to our entities. In fact, we could still be using `List` to represent the bag in the Java code (remember, there is no bags collection in Java). The actual difference appears in the mapping side. Instead of declaring the collection as a `list`, we use `bag`.

See the following mapping definition, with no changes to entities:

```
<hibernate-mapping package="com.madhusudhan.jh.collections.bags">
  <class name="Showroom" table="SHOWROOM_BAGS">
    <id column="SHOWROOM_ID" name="id">
      <generator class="native"/>
    </id>
    ...
      <bag name="cars" cascade="all" table="CARS_LIST">
      <key column="SHOWROOM_ID"/>
      <one-to-many class="Car"/>
    </bag>
  </class>
  <class name="Car" table="CARS_BAGS">
    ...
  </class>
</hibernate-mapping>
```

In the `bag` element, did you notice we dropped the index element that must exist in the `list` definition? In bags, the index of the collection is not persisted anymore; hence, you won't see the `index` element defined in the mapping.

Apart from this difference, the rest of the mechanics for running the tests is exactly the same as with lists. The test class defined here shows how we populate the data before persisting the entity:

```java
private void persist() {
    ...
    Showroom showroom = new Showroom();
    showroom.setLocation("East Croydon, Greater London");
    showroom.setManager("Barry Larry");

    // Define our cars - note their type
    String[] cars = new String[]{"Toyota","BMW","Citroen"};

    // Attach them to the showroom and persist
    showroom.setCars(cars);
    session.save(showroom);
    ...
}
```

 Bags are not a standard collection; they are Hibernate-specific. Although your code still uses java.util.List for a bag, the mapping needs to be explicit. It's better to stay away from bags if possible, and choose standard collections wherever you can.

In addition to bags, Hibernate supports *idbags*, a collection that provides a mechanism to have a surrogate key on the persisted collection itself, unlike bags where no key exists. As usual, the POJOs will not be changed, but the mapping deserves special attention:

```xml
<hibernate-mapping package="com.madhusudhan.jh.collections.idbags">
  <class name="Showroom" table="SHOWROOM_IDBAGS">
    <id column="SHOWROOM_ID" name="id">
      <generator class="native"/>
    </id>
    ...
      <idbag name="cars" cascade="all" table="SHOWROOM_CARS_IDBAGS">
      <collection-id  column="SHOWROOM_CAR_ID" type="long">
        <generator class="hilo"/>
      </collection-id>
      <key column="SHOWROOM_ID"/>
      <many-to-many class="Car" column="CAR_ID"/>
    </idbag>
  </class>
  <class name="Car" table="CARS_IDBAGS">
    <id column="CAR_ID" name="id">
      <generator class="native"/>
    </id>
    ...
  </class>
</hibernate-mapping>
```

Here we introduce the `idbags` element to represent our `cars` collection, pointing to a join table, SHOWROOM_CARS_IDBAGS. The `collection-id` element creates a primary key on the join table. In addition to its own primary key, the join table will also carry primary keys from the other two tables.

 The idbags collection is rarely used, so I would suggest you revisit your requirements should you wish to use it.

Persisting Collections Using Annotations

In the previous sections, we have seen the inner workings of saving collections using the XML mapping route. As an alternative, we can follow the annotations path for persisting the collections. The first thing we need to do is decorate the entities with the appropriate annotations. We'll enhance the car showroom example in this section.

There are two methods of preparing our code for annotations: using a foreign key or using an intermediary join table. We'll cover both of them next.

Using a Foreign Key

As we know, each showroom will have many cars, as represented by a one-to-many association. The `Showroom` entity consists of the collection of cars, showcasing them to customers. The cars, on the other hand, *belong* to a showcase; hence, are modeled to have a foreign key relationship to the showroom.

Let's first see the `Showroom` entity, which is defined as follows:

```
@Entity(name="SHOWROOM_LIST_ANN")
@Table(name="SHOWROM_LIST_ANN")
public class Showroom {
  @Id
  @Column(name="SHOWROOM_ID")
  @GeneratedValue(strategy=GenerationType.AUTO)
  private int id = 0;

  @OneToMany
  @JoinColumn(name="SHOWROOM_ID")
  @Cascade(CascadeType.ALL)
  private List<Car> cars = null;

  // other properties
  private String manager = null;
  private String location = null;
```

The class is declared as a persistable entity (via the @Entity annotation) mapping to a table identified with the @Table annotation. We define the identifier using an autogeneration strategy, meaning the identifier is set by one of the database's functions, such as auto_increment or identity.

Let's focus on one important property of the showroom: the collection of cars represented by a variable called cars. We use a java.util.List collection to hold the cars data. This variable is decorated with the @OneToMany annotation because each showroom will have many cars, and each car belongs to a showroom.

We learned earlier that the cars collection will have its own table with a foreign key referring to the showroom table's primary key (SHOWROOM_ID, in this case).

To let Hibernate know about this dependency, we declare the cars variable along with an @JoinColumn annotation defining the foreign key. We must provide the column name SHOWROOM_ID to pick up the list of cars from the cars table. The @Cascade annotation enables Hibernate to persist the collections associated with the main instance.

The Car entity is simple and straightforward:

```
@Entity(name="CAR_LIST_ANN")
@Table(name="CAR_LIST_ANN")
public class Car {
  @Id
  @GeneratedValue(strategy= GenerationType.AUTO)
  @Column(name="CAR_ID")
  private int id;
  private String name = null;
  private String color = null;
  ...
}
```

Here are the showroom and car database table scripts:

```
-- Table for showroom.
CREATE TABLE showroom_list_ann (
  SHOWROOM_ID int(10) NOT NULL AUTO_INCREMENT,
  location varchar(255) DEFAULT NULL,
  manager varchar(255) DEFAULT NULL,
  PRIMARY KEY (SHOWROOM_ID)
)
-- Table for cars
CREATE TABLE car_list_ann (
  CAR_ID int(11) NOT NULL AUTO_INCREMENT,
  color varchar(255) DEFAULT NULL,
  name varchar(255) DEFAULT NULL,
  SHOWROOM_ID int(11) DEFAULT NULL,
  PRIMARY KEY (CAR_ID),
  FOREIGN KEY (SHOWROOM_ID) REFERENCES showroom_list_ann (SHOWROOM_ID)
)
```

The cars table has its own primary key (CAR_ID) plus a foreign key (SHOWROOM_ID) referring to the main table.

Prepare your test case, adding the annotated classes to the configuration, as shown here:

```
Configuration config = new Configuration()
.configure("collections/list/ann/hibernate.cfg.xml")
.addAnnotatedClass(Showroom.class)
.addAnnotatedClass(Car.class);
```

As the client's persist mechanism won't be any different from what we saw when persisting lists, we will not repeat the test case here.

The output of the showroom is as follows:

```
Showroom{id=1, manager=Barry Larry, location=East Croydon, Greater London,
cars=[Car{id=1, name=Toyota, color=Racing Green},
Car{id=2, name=Nissan, color=White},
Car{id=3, name=BMW, color=Black},
Car{id=4, name=Mercedes, color=Silver}]]}
```

Now that we have seen how to persist collections using a foreign key, let's explore the second method: using a join table.

Using a Join Table

When using a *join table* strategy, we must have a mapping (join) table, which is an intermediary table holding the primary keys from both tables. For example, the following join table consists of primary keys from both showroom and cars:

```
// Join Table for showrooms and cars
SHOWROOM_ID            CAR_ID
1                      1
1                      2
2                      1
2                      2
```

Make the following alterations to the Showroom entity, annotating the cars table as appropriate:

```
@Entity(name="SHOWROOM_SET_ANN_JOINTABLE")
@Table(name="SHOWROOM_SET_ANN_JOINTABLE")
public class Showroom {
  @Id
  @Column(name="SHOWROOM_ID")
  @GeneratedValue(strategy=GenerationType.AUTO)
  private int id = 0;
  private String manager = null;
  private String location = null;

  @OneToMany
  @JoinTable
  (name="SHOWROOM_CAR_SET_ANN_JOINTABLE",
```

```
    joinColumns = @JoinColumn(name="SHOWROOM_ID")
    )
    @Cascade(CascadeType.ALL)
    private Set<Car> cars = null;
    ...
}
```

The @JoinTable annotation in the preceding snippet indicates that we will be using an intermediary table (SHOWROOM_CAR_SET_ANN_JOINTABLE, in this case). Also, note that cars are fetched using the SHOWROOM_ID join column.

The join table that is created is as follows:

```
CREATE TABLE showroom_car_set_ann_jointable (
    SHOWROOM_ID int(11) NOT NULL,
    car_id int(11) NOT NULL,
    PRIMARY KEY (SHOWROOM_ID,car_id),
    FOREIGN KEY (SHOWROOM_ID) REFERENCES showroom_set_ann_jointable (SHOWROOM_ID),
    FOREIGN KEY (car_id) REFERENCES car_set_ann_jointable (id)
)
```

As expected, the primary key is the combination of showroom_id and car_id. Also, notice that we have defined the foreign keys from the individual tables for showroom and car.

Summary

In this chapter, we have run through the various parts of persisting collections using the Hibernate framework. We have walked through the entities and their mappings in detail. We worked through examples of lists, sets, array lists, bags, and maps. We wrapped up by exploring how to persist the collections using annotations.

CHAPTER 5

Associations

In the object persistence world, understanding associations and relationships is essential. If we cannot handle complexity, we cannot solve real-life problems. In this chapter, we'll concentrate on the fundamentals of associations and their mappings. You'll also learn about the directionality and multiplicity of these associations.

In life, simplicity is not always the case! Objects cannot just linger on their own; they need to be able to associate with other objects representing real-life problems and solutions. Until now, we have seen how to persist and access simple Java objects such as a single Movie or Trade. If you dig in deep, a movie rarely exists without content—story, script, actors, and technicians, to name a few examples. The same is true about a trade: it's always associated with an underlying counterparty, quantity, reference data, and so on. These associations are crucial and need to be accounted for when we are persisting and retrieving data from a relational database. This is a humongous task for any ORM tool. Hibernate implements this functionality with elegance. The real power of Hibernate comes from its ability to help us manage these associations and relationships.

Associations

Understanding the associations between Java objects is crucial to working with Hibernate. Representing these associations in Java is quite straightforward: we use a class's attributes (variables) to do so. You may have already been working with associations without realizing it. Check out the following definition of two simple classes, Car and Engine:

```java
// Car class
public class Car {
  private int id;
  // Car has an engine - an association!
  private Engine engine;
  ...
```

```
  }

  // Engine class
  public class Engine {
    private int id = 0;
    private String make = null;
    ...
  }
```

We are defining a Car POJO with engine as an attribute. So, this code is indicating that the Car class is *associated* with the Engine class. In Java, we use the attributes to form associations with objects.

Before we move on, there's another term that you should understand: *relationships*. Relationships are associations between relational database tables. The relationships between the tables are expressed mostly through primary/foreign keys and other constraints.

 Although the terms *association* and *relationship* are often used interchangeably, I prefer to use *associations* when discussing objects and *relationships* when talking about tables.

When we talk about associations, there are two things that we should keep in mind: *multiplicity* and *directionality*.

Multiplicity

Multiplicity refers to *how many* of the specific objects are related to *how many* of the other target objects. We all may have one bank account, or more, or even none. Our neighbor may have one or more children (or none).

Whenever we are working with associations and relationships, we must think of them from the multiplicity angle too. Let's revisit the example of a car and its engine. Every car has an engine, and each engine belongs to one car. In simple words, this statement translates to "one" car has "one" engine. So, here the multiplicity is expressed as a *one-to-one* association.

Consider another example: a simplistic movie may consist of several actors. Here, as "one" movie consists of "one or more (i.e., many)" actors, the multiplicity is expressed as a *one-to-many* association (ideally, these actors would act in other movies, making it *many-to-many*, but for our example, we ignore that fact!).

The last one of the multiplicity associations is *many-to-many*: a student can enroll in *many* (zero or more) courses, while each course can consist of *many* students. In this context, *many* means zero, one, or more (not necessarily a large number).

So, in essence, there are three types of associations, as shown in Table 5-1.

Table 5-1. Types of associations

Association	Definition	Example
One-to-one	Each record in one table is related to exactly one record in the second table and vice versa. The other side could also be a zero record.	A car has only one engine.
One-to-many or many-to-one	Each record in one table is related to zero or more records in the second table.	A movie has many actors (one-to-many); an actor can act in many movies (many-to-one).
Many-to-many	Each record in either of the tables is related to zero or more records in the other table.	Each student can enroll in multiple courses, and each course can have many students registered.

Directionality

The other facet of association is directionality. This property defines the direction to which the association is tending. For example, in a Car and Engine association, by querying Car's attribute, we can figure out the engine; that is if you give me a Car object, I can tell you what engine it has. Take another example of a student attending university. By querying the courses attribute on the Student object, we could tell what courses he's enrolled in.

The associations can be either *unidirectional* or *bidirectional*. So, in the car and engine example, we can get the make of the engine if we are provided with the car data. However, if I provide you with the engine details, would you be able to tell me the car model? Unfortunately, we can't get the car details from the engine. This type of association is *unidirectional*: the directionality is one-sided only. In Java, we create a reference of the target object in the source class but not the other way. In the Car and Engine snippets shown previously, you can see that Car has a reference to an engine, but the Engine class does not have a reference to a car (hence it can't get a car for you!).

On the other hand, if we can navigate from source object to target object or vice versa, that relationship is said to be *bidirectional*. In the case of Car and Owner, we can derive the owner of the car given the Car object, as well as the owner's car given the Owner object. See the following definition of Owner and Car:

```
// Owner class
public class Owner {
  private int id = 0;
  // A Car that I own.
  // we could have a list of cars that owner owns too
  // but for simplicity's sake, let's take a single car
  private Car car = null;
  ...
}
```

```
// Car class
public class Car {
  private int id = 0;
  // my owner
  private Owner owner = null;
  ...
}
```

So, basically, what we are doing here is providing a reference of Car in the Owner object and a reference of Owner in the Car object to maintain a bidirectional association.

Let's throw multiplicity in this mix. The preceding example is a *one-to-one bidirectional* association.

How about a many-to-many bidirectional association? The student and course example exhibits this association. We can derive a student's courses from the Student object. At the same time, we can also deduce the list of students enrolled in a particular course by querying the Course object. This is defined in the Student and Course snippets shown here:

```
// Student class
public class Student {
    private int id = 0;
        // list of courses student is enrolled in
    private List<Course> courses = null;
    ...
}
// Course class
public class Course {
    private int id = 0;
        // list of students enrolled in this course
    private List<Student> students = null;
    ...
}
```

Did you notice that both classes have a reference to each other plus collection variables? This is the way we express many-to-many association with bidirectionality.

Now that we have a basic understanding of associations, let's see how they can be developed and implemented in Java one by one.

One-to-One Association

Using our Car and Engine example, we develop a one-to-one bidirectional association in this section. To recap, we know that every car will have one engine (we are not talking about those exotic twin-engine sports cars!) and every engine is fitted to a car; hence, they exhibit one-to-one mapping.

There are two ways of establishing a one-to-one association: using a primary key and using a foreign key. This difference is not apparent in the object model but is evident in our relational model. We'll go through both ways here. The persistent entities will be the same in both cases, so let's start defining them first.

The following snippets define the relevant `Car` and `Engine` classes:

```
// Car class
public class Car {
  private int id;
  private String name;
  private String color;
  // car has an engine
  private Engine engine;
  ...
}
// Engine class
public class Engine {
  private int id = 0;
  private String make = null;
  private String model = null;
  private String size = null;
  // this engine is fitted to a car
  private Car car = null;
}
```

Did you notice the references of `Car` in the `Engine` class and `Engine` in the `Car` class as engine and car references? This is the way we express our associations in the Java language.

Now that object modeling is out of our way, let's consider the table schemas.

As mentioned earlier, we have couple of choices to express the one-to-one relationship: using either a primary key or a foreign key. For both options, while the Java classes remain the same, the table definitions differ.

Using a Primary Key

The basic idea is that both tables exhibit the one-to-one relationship by sharing the same primary key. The tables are designed to share the primary key, as shown in the following snippet:

```
// CAR table
CREATE TABLE CAR (
  CAR_ID int(10) NOT NULL,
  NAME varchar(20) DEFAULT NULL,
  COLOR varchar(20) DEFAULT NULL,
  PRIMARY KEY (CAR_ID))

// ENGINE table
CREATE TABLE ENGINE (
  CAR_ID int(10) NOT NULL,
  SIZE varchar(20) DEFAULT NULL,
```

```
    MAKE varchar(20) DEFAULT NULL,
    MODEL varchar(20) DEFAULT NULL,
    PRIMARY KEY (CAR_ID),
    FOREIGN KEY (CAR_ID) REFERENCES car (CAR_ID))
```

The CAR table is straightforward, with a CAR_ID as the primary key. However, the interesting bits are in the ENGINE table. Two things you should have noticed there:

- The primary key of the ENGINE is a CAR_ID.
- It has a foreign key constraint pointing to the primary key of the CAR table. So, an engine will always be created with the same id as that of a car. Thus, we say both tables share the same primary key.

Now let's see how we do mapping for a one-to-one association. The mapping for the Car object against the CAR table is given here, in a *Car.hbm.xml* file:

```
<hibernate-mapping package="com.madhusudhan.jh.associations.one2one">
  <class name="Car" table="CAR">
    <id name="id" column="CAR_ID">
      <generator class="assigned"/>
    </id>
    <property name="name" column="NAME"/>
    <property name="color" column="COLOR"/>
    <one-to-one name="engine" class="Engine" cascade="all"/>
  </class>
</hibernate-mapping>
```

By now, this mapping should be familiar to you.

The id is set by the application, and the relevant properties are mapped to the table columns. Did you notice how the engine property was set? A one-to-one mapping tag is used to associate the engine to the Car. What this notation is truly saying is:

- The instance of the Car (it is defined for the Car class) has a property called engine.
- Car and Engine exhibit a one-to-one association.
- Engine is set by values pulled from the ENGINE table (which is mapped to the Engine object).

The Engine mapping is a bit more involved, however:

```
<hibernate-mapping package="com.madhusudhan.jh.associations.one2one">
    <class name="Engine" table="ENGINE">
    <id name="id" column="CAR_ID" >
      <generator class="foreign">
        <param name="property">car</param>
      </generator>
    </id>
    <one-to-one name="car" class="Car" constrained="true"/>
    <property name="size" column="SIZE"/>
```

```
    ...
  </class>
</hibernate-mapping>
```

We know that Engine's primary key (id) is the same as Car's id. We should somehow mention this fact in our mapping to let Hibernate know how to deal with this situation. There is a special generator class called foreign for such purposes. This generator checks for a property named car (which is defined via the one-to-one tag further down in the mapping) and picks up the id from that reference.

There's one more attribute we've used in the one-to-one element: constrained="true". Simply put, this means that the primary key of the ENGINE table has a foreign key constraint, which is deduced from the primary key of the CAR table.

The hard work is done, so let's test the application.

Testing the Association

To demonstrate how this relationship works, we will create a test class as shown here:

```
/* Test for one-to-one mapping using shared primary key */
public class OneToOneTest {
  ...
  private void persist() {
    ...
    // First create an instance of Car, set id and other properties
    Car car = new Car();

    // Remember, we are using application generator for ids
    car.setId(1);
    car.setName("Cadillac ATS Sedan");
    car.setColor("White");

    // Next, create an instance of engine and set values.
    // Note: you are not setting the id!
    Engine engine = new Engine();
    engine.setMake("V8 Series");
    engine.setModel("DTS");
    engine.setSize("1.6 V8 GAS");

    // Now we associate them together using the setter on the car
    car.setEngine(engine);
    engine.setCar(car);

        // Lastly, we are persisting them
    session.save(car);
    session.save(engine);
        ...
  }
}
```

Although the code is doing lots of things, it is not difficult to grasp (read the comments to understand the operations). Note that the primary key of the Engine is not set on the object while we're creating it. This is because we are borrowing and sharing the id from the Car. This way, during the process of creating the Engine, Hibernate grabs the id from the car and sets it onto the Engine object.

We are persisting both the car and engine in the preceding code. They are pretty much individual tables in this scenario except with primary-foreign key constraints. In our next case, we will see how the engine gets persisted by just persisting the car.

Tables 5-2 and 5-3 show the output from the tables.

Table 5-2. Car table

CAR_ID	COLOR	NAME
1	White	Cadillac ATS Sedan

Table 5-3. Engine table

CAR_ID	SIZE	MAKE	MODEL
1	1.6	V8 Gas	V8

We can see that the primary key CAR_ID is shared across both tables.

Using a Foreign Key

To use the foreign key strategy, we have to alter the table and mapping definitions (the POJOs remain the same). Modified table definitions are given here (note that the table names have been modified with the suffix V2 so they won't clash with our earlier incarnations):

```
CREATE TABLE CAR_V2 (
  CAR_ID int(10) NOT NULL,
  ENGINE_ID int(10) NOT NULL,
  COLOR varchar(20) DEFAULT NULL,
  NAME varchar(20) DEFAULT NULL,
  PRIMARY KEY (CAR_ID),
  CONSTRAINT FK_ENG_ID FOREIGN KEY (engine_id) REFERENCES ENGINE_v2 (ENGINE_ID)
)

CREATE TABLE ENGINE_V2 (
  ENGINE_ID int(10) NOT NULL,
  MAKE varchar(20) DEFAULT NULL,
  MODEL varchar(20) DEFAULT NULL,
  SIZE varchar(20) DEFAULT NULL,
  PRIMARY KEY (ENGINE_ID)
)
```

The ENGINE_V2 definition is simple and sweet; it's a normal table with a primary key ENGINE_ID. The notable change is in the CAR_V2 table: in addition to having its own primary key (CAR_ID), it also has a foreign key (ENGINE_ID) that points to the ENGINE_V2 table.

The next step is to define the mappings. The Engine mapping shouldn't be any surprise to you:

```
<hibernate-mapping package="com.madhusudhan.jh.associations.one2one">
    <!-- using foreign key -->
    <class name="Engine" table="ENGINE_V2">
    <id name="id" column="ENGINE_ID" >
      <generator class="assigned"/>
    </id>
    <property name="size" column="SIZE" />
    ...
  </class>
</hibernate-mapping>
```

We define the application strategy for setting the id of the object and map the properties of the class to the relevant table columns. The next snippet is the mapping for the Car object:

```
<hibernate-mapping package="com.madhusudhan.jh.associations.one2one">
  <class name="Car" table="CAR_V2">
    <id name="id" column="CAR_ID" >
      <generator class="assigned"/>
    </id>
    <property name="name" column="NAME" />
    <property name="color" column="COLOR"/>
    <!-- the unique="true" makes this many-to-one
        relationship as one-to-one.
        This is very important setting for this strategy -->

    <many-to-one name="engine" class="Engine"
          column="engine_id"
          unique="true"
          cascade="all" />
  </class>
</hibernate-mapping>
```

Note the use of the many-to-one element (instead of the one-to-one element we've used in the earlier case) with the additional attribute unique="true". By setting this attribute, we are essentially converting a many-to-one relationship to a one-to-one association. This attribute will ensure that one Car is associated to one Engine!

Let's modify the test client to reflect the changes:

```
private void persistV2() {
  // Create an Engine
  Engine e = new Engine();
```

```
        e.setId(1);
        e.setMake("V8 Series");
        e.setModel("DTS");
        e.setSize("1.6 V8 GAS");

        // Create a Car
        Car car = new Car();
        car.setId(1);
        car.setName("Cadillac ATS Sedan");
        car.setColor("White");

        // Associate both
        car.setEngine(e);

        // Now persist the car using the save method.

        // Note: The Engine gets saved automatically because of the cascade attribute
        // defined in the mapping

        session.save(car);
        ...
    }
```

From the preceding code, you can see that we are creating both entities, Engine and Car, respectively. We then add an engine to the car and save it to the database. Notice that we are *not* saving the engine explicitly. That's because, when the car is persisted, its associated objects (engine, in this case) are saved too because of the cascade="all" attribute defined in the mapping file.

Before we wrap up the discussion on one-to-one associations, you may be wondering what's the preferred approach? I personally prefer the foreign key relationship by using the many-to-one element with the unique attribute set to true. In fact, Hibernate recommends this approach too.

Annotations

When you're using annotations, you should mark up the POJOs. The Car entity is defined as shown here:

```
    @Entity
    @Table(name="CAR_ONE2ONE_ANN")
    public class Car {
      @Id
      @Column(name="CAR_ID")
      @GeneratedValue(strategy= GenerationType.AUTO)
      private int id;

      private String name = null;

      @OneToOne (cascade= CascadeType.ALL)
```

```
@JoinColumn(name="ENGINE_ID")
private Engine engine = null;
...
```

The Car class is annotated with an @Entity, making it eligible for persistence. The @Id annotation is declared on the id field pointing to the CAR_ID from the table. We declare the one-to-one mapping using the @OneToOne annotation. As we have to join the car to the ENGINE table, the @JoinColumn is used on the ENGINE_ID column.

The Engine class is much simpler. Apart from the usual class-level declarations, such as the @Entity and @Table annotations, the relevant annotation is on the car field (@One ToOne):

```
@Entity
@Table(name="ENGINE_ONE2ONE_ANN")
public class Engine {
  @Id
  @Column(name="ENGINE_ID")
  @GeneratedValue(strategy= GenerationType.AUTO)
  private int id = 0;
  @OneToOne(mappedBy="car")
  private Car car = null;
  ...
```

Add these two AJOs during your session factory initialization, and off you go to test the functionality.

Now that we have seen one-to-one in action, the next section explores the many-to-one (or one-to-many) association.

Bear in mind, as we have already discussed one-to-one association in depth, the rest of the associations differ only a bit. We won't go through the rest in detail, as the concepts apply for all the associations. We mostly concentrate on any differences among the associations in the next few sections.

One-to-Many (or Many-to-One) Association

The relationship between a movie and actors is a one-to-many association: one movie consists of many actors. Actually, we have already dealt with this relationship in an earlier section, so we'll only skim it here.

Let's work with the POJOs first:

```
// Actor
public class Actor {
  private int id = 0;
  private String firstName = null;
  private String lastName = null;
  private String shortName = null;
  // Setters and getters
```

```
  ...
  }
}
```

Because we are looking at the unidirectional relationship, the `Actor` POJO will not have any reference to the `Movie` object. We will see the bidirectional relationship in a minute.

The `Movie` POJO will look like the following:

```java
public class Movie {
  private int id = 0;
  private String title = null;
  private Set<Actor> actors = null;
  public Set<Actor> getActors() {
     return actors;
  }
  public void setActors(Set<Actor> actors) {
    this.actors = actors;
  }
  ...
}
```

The important bit is the `actors` variable. A movie consists of several actors, so we have declared the `Movie` object to have a `Set` of actors.

Before we jump to the mapping files, let's look at the database scripts for the relevant tables. Remember, the `Actors` table will contain a foreign key pointing to the movie's primary key:

```sql
// Simple and straightforward movie definition
CREATE TABLE MOVIE_ONE2MANY (
  MOVIE_ID int(10) NOT NULL,
  TITLE varchar(10) DEFAULT NULL,
  PRIMARY KEY (MOVIE_ID)
)
// Note that foreign key definition
CREATE TABLE ACTOR_ONE2MANY (
  ACTOR_ID int(10) NOT NULL AUTO_INCREMENT,
  FIRST_NAME varchar(20) DEFAULT NULL,
  LAST_NAME varchar(20) DEFAULT NULL,
  SHORT_NAME varchar(20) DEFAULT NULL,
  MOVIE_ID int(10) DEFAULT NULL,
  PRIMARY KEY (ACTOR_ID),
  CONSTRAINT FK_MOV_ID FOREIGN KEY (MOVIE_ID)
  REFERENCES MOVIE_ONE2MANY (MOVIE_ID)
)
```

The `MOVIE_ONE2MANY` table is straightforward, whereas in the `ACTOR_ONE2MANY` table, we define a foreign key relationship pointing to the primary key of the MOVIES table.

The last piece is the mapping declarations. The reverse of the table relationship holds here; that is, we can traverse from movie to actors or vice versa. The `Actor` definition is straightforward, while the `Movie` object maintains the association:

```
<hibernate-mapping package="com.madhusudhan.jh.associations.one2many">
  <class name="Actor" table="ACTOR_ONE2MANY">
    <id  name="id" column="ACTOR_ID">
      <generator class="assigned"/>
    </id>
    <property name="firstName" column="FIRST_NAME" />
        ...
  </class>
</hibernate-mapping>

// Movie
<hibernate-mapping package="com.madhusudhan.jh.associations.one2many">
  <class name="Movie" table="MOVIE_ONE2MANY">
    <id name="id" column="MOVIE_ID" >
      <generator class="assigned"/>
    </id>
    <property name="title" column="TITLE" />
        <set name="actors" table="ACTOR_ONE2MANY" cascade="all">
        <key column="MOVIE_ID" not-null="true"/>
        <one-to-many class="Actor"/>
    </set>
  </class>
</hibernate-mapping>
```

We define a `set` element to represent the actors association. This is equivalent to the `java.util.Set` we've defined in our `Movie` POJO. What the preceding code says is that for each movie, fetch the actors from the `ACTOR_ONE2MANY` table associated by the `Actor` class by querying with a `MOVIE_ID` key.

Create a test case to see the one-to-many mapping in action:

```
public class OneToManyTest {
  private Movie persistMovie() {
    Movie movie = null;
    Actor actor = null;
        Set<Actor> actors = new HashSet<Actor>();
        // Create actors - during the time of writing this example,
    // I was watching the movie Chennai Express :)

    actor = new Actor("Sharukh", "Khan", "King Khan");
    actors.add(actor);

    actor = new Actor("Deepika", "Padukone", "Miss Chennai");
    actors.add(actor);

    // Create the Movie object and associate actors
    movie = new Movie("Chennai Express");
    movie.setActors(actors);
```

```
        session.save(movie);
    ...
    }
}
```

The operations are not convoluted: create a new `Movie` object and associate the `Actors` to it. We save the movie and the collection of actors will get persisted automatically due to the `cascade=all` setting.

In the preceding example, with the actors information, we can't fetch their movies because the relationship is not bidirectional. Implementing the bidirectional association requires a couple of changes in our POJOs and mapping (the tables will remain as they are).

Bidirectional One-to-Many Association

In `Actor`, we need to add a reference pointing to a `Movie` object, as shown in the following (there is no change to the `Movie` POJO—this already has the reference to the actors anyway!):

```
public class Actor {
        // We want to know the movie this actor belongs to!
    private Movie movie = null;
        ...
        public Movie getMovie() {
        return movie;
    }
        public void setMovie(Movie movie) {
        this.movie = movie;
    }
}
```

The next change is to the *Actor.hbm.xml* (mapping) file; it will now have a `many-to-one` mapping element:

```
<hibernate-mapping package="com.madhusudhan.jh.associations.one2many.bi">
  <class name="Actor" table="ACTOR_ONE2MANY_BI">
    <id  name="id" column="ACTOR_ID">
      <generator class="assigned"/>
    </id>
    <many-to-one name="movie" column="MOVIE_ID" class="Movie"/>
        ...
  </class>
</hibernate-mapping>
```

The `many-to-one` element indicates the "many" side of the `Actor` class. Now, not only can you get to actors via your `Movie` object, but you can also find the movie in which an actor appeared, by calling the `actor.getMovie` access method. This establishes a bidirectional relationship between movie and actors.

___

Many-to-Many Association

The many-to-many association establishes a relationship between two classes in such a way that each source-side class will have many of the target-side classes, and vice versa. In the example of Student and Course, the relationship can be many-to-many: a student can take many courses, while a course may consist of many students. In fact, the previous example of Movie and Actor is, strictly speaking, many-to-many: a movie will have many actors, while an actor performs in many movies (for simplicity, however, we considered that association one-to-many in the preceding section).

So, how does many-to-many look on the Java side? As you may have already guessed, both sides will have an attribute representing a collection with access methods. While in the database, a third table—usually called a link table—is used to link the many-to-many mapping.

The POJOs will have attributes referencing each other, as shown here:

```java
// Course class
public class Course {
  private int id = 0;
  private String title = null;
  // Collection hold Students
  private Set<Student> students = null;
  ...
}
// Student class
public class Student {
  private int id = 0;
  private String name = null;
  // Student enrolled in multiple courses
  private Set<Course> courses = null;
  ...
}
```

As you can see, we are creating a bidirectional many-to-many association between the Student and Course classes. The relevant mappings are:

```xml
<!-- Student Mapping-->
<hibernate-mapping package="com.madhusudhan.jh.associations.many2many">
  <class name="Student" table="STUDENT">
      ...
        <set name="courses" table="STUDENT_COURSE" cascade="all">
      <key column="STUDENT_ID" />
      <many-to-many column="COURSE_ID" class="Course"/>
    </set>
  </class>
</hibernate-mapping>

<!-- Course Mapping-->
<hibernate-mapping package="com.madhusudhan.jh.associations.many2many">
  <class name="Course" table="COURSE">
```

```
    ...
    <set name="students" table="STUDENT_COURSE" inverse="true" cascade="all">
        <key column="COURSE_ID" />
        <many-to-many column="STUDENT_ID" class="Student"/>
    </set>
  </class>
</hibernate-mapping>
```

The last part is the task of creating the link table; the script is as follows:

```
CREATE TABLE student_course (
    COURSE_ID int(10) NOT NULL,
    STUDENT_ID int(10) NOT NULL,
    PRIMARY KEY (COURSE_ID,STUDENT_ID),
    CONSTRAINT fk_course_id FOREIGN KEY (COURSE_ID) REFERENCES course (COURSE_ID),
    CONSTRAINT fk_student_id FOREIGN KEY (STUDENT_ID) REFERENCES student
        (STUDENT_ID)
)
```

Summary

In this chapter, we learned about object associations in detail. We looked at different associations: one-to-one, one-to-many (or many-to-one), and many-to-many. We also discussed multiplicity and directionality over the course of a few examples.

CHAPTER 6

Advanced Concepts

In the previous chapters, you learned about the basics of Hibernate. Hibernate is a feature-rich ORM framework, so a discussion of all its offerings would take reams of paper. However, there are a few features that are important for any developer working with Hibernate to understand. This chapter describes the features that are particularly useful if you are looking to get more out of your framework. The concepts discussed here will enable you to extend the framework to suit your application needs.

Hibernate Types

In our mapping files, we declared the mapping of an object's property to a table column as `property column="COLOR" name="color"`. However, how does Hibernate know the COLOR column is a VARCHAR and the color property is a `String` type?

Well, Hibernate uses Java's reflection to find out the type of the property. Although this option of omitting the types works out fine, the preferred and recommended option is to set the types on the properties implicitly. Setting `property column="COLOR" name="color" type="string"` explicitly will easily give Hibernate the property's type.

Did you notice that we declared the type of the color property as `string` but not `String`? The `string` type is neither a Java type nor a SQL type; in fact, it is Hibernate's own type. Hibernate has extensive support for types, including built-in types such as string, boolean, and integer, as well as our own predefined custom types.

Entity and Value Types

Types are essentially categorized as entity and value types. The main difference is that while entity types have an identifier and exist on their own, value types do not. Our persistent objects, such as `Movie`, `Car`, `Showroom`, and `Student`—are examples of entities. They have an identifier to uniquely represent them, which makes them independent.

Value types, on the other hand, cannot exist on their own; they are dependent on other objects like entities.

Hibernate provides two categories of value types, basic types and components:

Basic types
> Basic types are used to map a table column to a Java property. For example, earlier we saw the `string` type mapping to the `title` of a `Movie` object. The `string`, `boolean`, `int`, `long`, `double`, `timestamp`, and other types fall under this category. As you can imagine, they have to be associated to an entity (`Movie`, in this case) to exist.

Components
> Sometimes we wish to have a type defined based on more than one field. The component type defines a set of fields as a specific type. For example, we may wish to represent a phone number as an aggregation of country code, region number, and a name. We may need to use this combination of composite columns/attributes over and over again, so it would be efficient to develop a `PhoneNumber` component and associate it as a type. Components are quite handy for splitting table data into varied objects. We will discuss components further in the coming sections.

Java collections also form a persistent type; refer to Chapter 4 for more details on this subject.

Custom Types

In addition to these types, Hibernate also provides excellent support for creating our own type. If our requirement is to use the `PhoneNumber` type we just discussed, first we need to create a type. We'll call this the `PhoneNumberType` class; it implements Hibernate's own interfaces, such as `org.hibernate.type.Type` or its derived variants (`BasicType`).

In the following example, we create a `PhoneNumberType` class that implements the `org.hibernate.type.BasicType` interface. There are quite a few methods that need implementation, but only a couple of them are shown in the following snippet for brevity's sake:

```
public class PhoneNumberType implements BasicType {
  public int[] sqlTypes() {
    return new int[]{
      IntegerType.INSTANCE.sqlType(),
      IntegerType.INSTANCE.sqlType(),
      StringType.INSTANCE.sqlType()
    };
  }
  public Class returnedClass() {
    return PhoneNumber.class;
  }
  ...
}
```

The `sqlTypes` method lets Hibernate know that our type is made of two integers (country code and region number) and a string (the name). The next bit tells Hibernate about our new type by registering it. We do this in the following code, by invoking the `registerTypeOverride` method on the `Configuration` instance:

```
Configuration config =
  new Configuration().configure("/types/hibernate.cfg.xml");
config.registerTypeOverride(new PhoneNumberType());
```

Once we have the type defined, we can use it in our mapping as one property of the class. For example:

```
<class name="CustomCar" table="CUSTOM_CAR">
  ...
  <property name="phoneNumber" column="PHONE_NUMBER"
  type="com.madhusudhan.jh.advanced.types.PhoneNumberType"/>
  ...
</class>
```

We have just scratched the surface of types here. If you'd like further information on types, refer to the online Hibernate manuals.

Components

Sometimes we wish to organize objects according to the object model rather than depending on a table. It wouldn't be a good design if we had one big object with 100 properties representing all 100 columns of a table!

Consider the `Person` class listed here:

```
public class Person {
  private String firstName = null;
  private String nickName = null;
  private String lastName = null;

  // Phone details
  private int areaCode = 0;
  private int phoneNumber = 0;
  private String name = null;
}
```

Our person object has three properties related to phone number: an area code, phone number, and name. Let's say we have a new business requirement that a person can now have multiple phone numbers. If we stick with the preceding design, we need to add (duplicate!) another set of three properties. Do we keep repeating the properties every time we wish to define an additional address in the person object? We can get away from this poor design by refactoring the person object and creating a `PhoneNumber` class as follows:

```
public class PhoneNumber {
  // Phone details
  private int areaCode = 0;
  private int phoneNumber = 0;
  private String name = null;
}
```

So, the Person object now becomes:

```
public class Person {
  private String firstName = null;
  private String nickName = null;
  private String lastName = null;
  // Multiple phone details
  private PhoneNumber homePhone = null;
  private PhoneNumber mobilePhone = null;
}
```

That's simple refactoring, isn't it? We have refactored the Java entities—no suprise there. Did you notice we did not amend the table structure at all (i.e., you still have the three phone-related columns as they appeared earlier in the person table)?

How can we now create the mapping between the enhanced person object with the newly created PhoneNumber class? This is where components come into the picture. Components help us to *group* columns into our objects.

In the preceding example, the PhoneNumber is not an entity itself; it's merely a representation of a few table columns. There is a strict one-to-one parent-child relationship between the Person and PhoneNumber classes.

The mapping goes like this:

```
<class name="Person" table="PERSON">
  <id  name="id" column="PERSON_ID">
    <generator class="native"/>
  </id>
  <property name="firstName" column="FIRST_NAME" />
  ...
  <component name="homePhone" class="PhoneNumber">
    <property name="areaCode" column="HOME_AREA_CODE"/>
    <property name="phoneNumber" column="HOME_PHONE_NUMBER"/>
    <property name="name" column="HOME_NAME"/>
  </component>

  <component name="mobilePhone" class="PhoneNumber">
    <property name="areaCode" column="MOBILE_AREA_CODE"/>
    <property name="phoneNumber" column="MOBILE_PHONE_NUMBER"/>
    <property name="name" column="MOBILE_NAME"/>
  </component>
</class>
```

We use the component tag to represent the phoneNumber variable. Notice the class attribute referring to our actual PhoneNumber class and PhoneNumber attributes referring to the specific columns. In our Person code, we will have a phoneNumber variable that can be managed explicitly as if it were a single column. We defined two components, one for home phone and another for mobile phone.

We access the variables of the component via the standard format: person.getPhoneNumber().getName(), which is simple. Components are really useful for grouping fields into a fine-grained domain model.

Caching

When it comes to performance tuning, caching strategy tops the list. We can improve the performance of any data-intensive application by introducing caching mechanisms. Hibernate supports caching of persistent objects using first-level and second-level caching methods.

First-Level Caching

The first level is simply the transactional cache associated with the Session object, which is available during the lifespan of that session or in the conversation only. This caching is provided by default by the framework.

See the following code:

```
private void firstLevelCache() {
  ...
  int personId = 10;

  Person person = new Person();
  person.setId(personId);
  person.setFirstName("Madhusudhan");
  person.setLastName("Konda");

  session.save(person);

  // Let's load the same object to set the nickname
  // Note that we are using the same session

  person = (Person) session.load(Person.class, personId);
  person.setNickName("MK2");

  session.save(person);
}
```

In this listing, we first create an instance of Person and set the values on it before saving it. With the same session instance, we retrieve the person object again to set another attribute (nickName, in this case). When you load the object the second time, the object is retrieved from the cache maintained by the session itself, thus a network roundtrip to the database is avoided. The session cache is keyed with the class type, and hence you may have to take extra care when trying to override the existing instance.

Second-Level Caching

The second-level cache is globally available via the `SessionFactory` class. So, any data present in this cache is made available to the entire application.

Hibernate supports a few open source cache implementations, such as EhCache and InfiniSpan. However, should we need to provide our own, we can do so by implementing the `org.hibernate.cache.spi.CacheProvider` interface with a concrete implementation. EhCache is the default second-level cache provider in Hibernate.

To plug in the caching provider, set the property `hibernate.cache.provider_class`, referring to the appropriate cache provider. For example, the following listing demonstrates how to plug in JBoss's InifiniSpan as the cache provider:

```
<hibernate-configuration>
  <session-factory>
    <!-- Infinispan cache provider setting -->
    <property name="hibernate.cache.provider_class">
    org.hibernate.cache.infinispan.InfinispanRegionFactory
    </property>
    ...
  </session-factory>
</hibernate-configuration>
```

We can set the caching policy on individual classes that need to be cached by using various caching attributes. Check out the following code, which sets the `cache` attribute on the `class` tag in our mapping file:

```
<hibernate-mapping package="com.madhusudhan.jh.advanced.cache">
  <class name="Person" table="PERSON">
    <cache usage="read-write" region="" include="all"/>
    ...
  </class>
</hibernate-mapping>
```

The `usage` element is mandatory; it sets the caching concurrency strategy (`read-write` in the preceding example).

There are four settings that the `usage` attribute exposes:

`transactional`

This strategy provides support for cache implementation providers that support transactional caching. Note that not all the cache providers have transactional caching products available.

read-only

If we wish to have frequent reads of persistent objects, but no updates back to the durable storage space, then you should choose read-only. As it requires minimal or no writes to the database, performance with this option is strong.

read-write

This strategy enables both reading and writing of the objects to and from to the database.

nonstrict-read-write

This strategy supports a scenario in which the objects are not updated that often.

To turn on the option of caching globally, set the hibernate.cache.default_cache_concurrency_strategy property in your configuration file.

Caching Queries

Not only can we cache objects, we can cache queries too. If you have some queries that will be invoked quite often, it is advisable to cache them. To use this functionality, set the hibernate.cache.use_query_cache attribute to true.

We need to do one more thing in our code: set the cacheable property on the Query to true by invoking the Query.setCacheable() method.

Inheritance Strategies

When we think of object-oriented programming, one principle that comes immediately to mind is inheritance. We always think in terms of *has-a* or *is-a* relationships when modeling real-world problems. For example, Executive *is an* Employee and *has an* Address. Unfortunately, relational databases do not understand the is-a inheritance relationship, although we can get away with using primary and foreign keys for has-a inheritance support . This poses a subtle problem when the ORM tool tries to persist the inheritance relationships. Hibernate overcomes this problem by providing three different strategies to support inheritance persistence, each of which we'll explore in the following sections.

Table-per-Class Strategy

The table-per-class strategy, defines one table for all the object hierarchies. This is a simple strategy, as a single table suffices to store the application's data needs. For example, both the Employee and the Executive object's data is persisted in the same table.

But how can we segregate the data? How can we differentiate an employee's data from an an executive's? We do this by employing a *discriminator* column.

A discriminator column tags the data for each class separately. In the case of the Employee and Executive object model, there would be two rows in the same table with an additional column indicating each row as an employee or an executive. Table 6-1 illustrates.

Table 6-1. Table-per-class strategy

ID	NAME	ROLE	DISCRIMINATOR
5	Barry Bumbles	NULL	EMPLOYEE
6	Harry Dumbles	Operations	EXECUTIVE

There are two rows in the table; however, the discriminator column differentiates them accordingly based on its column value. The first row indicates that it's Employee's data, while the second is Executive's.

Let's see how we can implement this in Hibernate. We have two classes representing the Employee and Executive, with Executive extending the Employee class:

```
// The base class
public class Employee {
  private int id = 0;
  private String name = null;
  ...
}

// The child class
public class Executive extends Employee{
  private String role = null;
  ...
}
```

Table-per-class strategy using XML mapping

Now that we have the persistent classes, our next step is to define the mapping. See the following *EmployeeExecutive.hbm.xml* mapping file:

```
<hibernate-mapping package="com.madhusudhan.jh.advanced.inheritance.s1">
  <class name="Employee" table="INHERITANCE_S1_EMPLOYEE"
  discriminator-value="EMPLOYEE">
    <id  name="id" column="EMPLOYEE_ID">
      <generator class="native"/>
    </id>
    <discriminator column="DISCRIMINATOR" type="string"/>

    <property name="name" column="NAME" />
    <subclass name="Executive" extends="Employee"
    discriminator-value="EXECUTIVE">
        <property name="role" column="ROLE"/>
    </subclass>
```

```
        </class>
    </hibernate-mapping>
```

We declare the Employee class, pointing to the table as expected. Did you notice the discriminator-value tag defined on the class element? This is a static value that will be persisted with the employee object in a DISCRIMINATOR column. This column is described by another property called discriminator, which is declared just under the id element in the preceding snippet.

Now, the second step is to understand the mapping definition for the Executive class. We use the subclass element to indicate the hierarchy (see extends="Employee" in the definition). As with the Employee, we set a static value, "EXECUTIVE", for all persisted executive objects as defined by the discriminator-value.

For clarity's sake, see the following table definition:

```
create table inheritance_s1_employee(
employee_id     int not null auto_increment,
name                    varchar(20) not null,
role                    varchar(20),
discriminator   varchar(20),
primary key (employee_id));
```

Note the discriminator column on the table. It's simply a column to store the two values, EXECUTIVE or EMPLOYEE, defined in the mapping cofiguration.

Now that we have seen the table-per-class inheritance strategy using XML mapping, it's time to check out how we can use annotations with this strategy.

Table-per-class strategy using annotations

Table-per-class inheritance using annotations is straightforward. Create the parent class Employee with the following annotations:

```
@Entity(name="INHERITANCE_S1_EMPLOYEE_ANN")
@Inheritance(strategy=InheritanceType.SINGLE_TABLE)
@DiscriminatorColumn(name="DISCRIMINATOR"
    discriminatoryType=DicriminatorType.STRING)
@DiscriminatorValue(value="EMPLOYEE")

public class Employee {
  @Id
  @Column(name="EMPLOYEE_ID")
  private int id = 0;
  ...
}
```

We define the inheritance strategy by annotating our entity with the @Inheritance annotation. This annotation accepts a strategy via the strategy variable; in this case, it's a SINGLE_TABLE strategy. The InheritanceType also has TABLE_PER_CLASS and

JOINED strategies. Don't be tempted to set an InheritanceType.TABLE_PER_CLASS value when using th table-per-class strategy—we must set SINGLE_TABLE only. The TABLE_PER_CLASS is set for the table-per-*concrete*-class strategy, which we will see in a minute.

In addition to the inheritance strategy, we need to define the discriminator column (as discussed in the previous section) via the @DiscriminatorColumn annotation. This annotation describes the name and type of the discriminator column. The @DiscriminatorValue sets the static value on the entity (EMPLOYEE, in this case).

The subclass EMPLOYEE's annotations are simple:

```
@Entity
@DiscriminatorValue(value="EXECUTIVE")
public class Executive extends Employee {
  private String role = null;
  ...
}
```

As expected, the @DiscriminatorValue value sets the static value as EXECUTIVE on all of the persisted executive objects.

Now, the last piece is to attach the annotated classes via the configuration:

```
public class InheritanceStrategyOneTest {
  private void init() {
    Configuration config = new Configuration()
      .configure("advanced/inheritance/s1/hibernate.cfg.ann.xml")
      .addAnnotatedClass(Employee.class)
      .addAnnotatedClass(Executive.class);
      ...
  }
  private void test() {
    Employee emp = new Employee("Barry Bumbles");
    session.save(emp);
    Executive ex = new Executive("Harry Dumbles");
    ex.setRole("Director");
    session.save(ex);
      ...
  }
}
```

The preceding snippet demonstrates the table-per-class strategy for persisting the test data. This strategy is fine as long as we have a simple hierarchy. The minute we start having a deep-level object graph, it might grow out of proportion and be unsuitable to maintain. And if your domain classes change, the table will need alterations too. Note that you cannot declare NOT NULL constraints on the columns related to the subclasses if you choose this strategy.

Table-per-Subclass Strategy

In the previous section, we saw that the table-per-class strategy persisted all rows to a single table, differentiating each of the rows using a discriminating column. Instead of having one humongous table to store the object graphs, we have the option of a separate *table for each class*. This strategy is called the *table-per-subclass* inheritance persistence strategy.

In this strategy, all the subclasses (including the parent class if the parent class is not an abstract class) will have their own table persistence. Continuing with our employee-executive example, the employee and executive objects will be persisted to the EMPLOY EE and EXECUTIVE tables, respectively. Also, we will not be defining a discriminator column in this method. However, note that the subclass's tables will have to have a foreign key referring to the parent class's primary key.

Let's start developing an example to demonstrate the table-per-subclass strategy.

First, the database scripts:

```
// EMPLOYEE table
CREATE TABLE inheritance_s2_employee (
  EMPLOYEE_ID int(11) NOT NULL AUTO_INCREMENT,
  NAME varchar(255) DEFAULT NULL,
  PRIMARY KEY (EMPLOYEE_ID)
)
// EXECUTIVE table
CREATE TABLE inheritance_s2_executive (
  EMPLOYEE_ID int(11) NOT NULL,
  ROLE varchar(255) DEFAULT NULL,
  PRIMARY KEY (EMPLOYEE_ID),
  CONSTRAINT FK_EMP FOREIGN KEY (EMPLOYEE_ID)
  REFERENCES inheritance_s2_employee (EMPLOYEE_ID)
)
```

The EMPLOYEE table is a standard one, while the EXECUTIVE table (which represents our subclass Executive) has a constraint defined on it.

Table-per-subclass strategy using XML mapping

While the Employee and Executive class definitions won't change, as we still use the same object hierarchy, the mapping does change:

```
<hibernate-mapping package="com.madhusudhan.jh.advanced.inheritance.s2">
  <class name="Employee" table="INHERITANCE_S2_EMPLOYEE">
    <id  name="id" column="EMPLOYEE_ID">
      <generator class="native"/>
    </id>
    <property name="name" column="NAME" />
    <joined-subclass name="Executive" table="INHERITANCE_S2_EXECUTIVE">
        <key column="EMPLOYEE_ID"/>
        <property name="role" column="ROLE"/>
```

```
    </joined-subclass>
  </class>
</hibernate-mapping>
```

The main `Employee` (parent) class is defined as expected, but the `Executive` (child) class is tagged with a `joined-class` element. The subclass now has its own table (in this case, `INHERITANCE_S2_EXECUTIVE`). Also, notice how the foreign key is being tied up by using the key attribute in a `joined-subclass`.

That's all we need to do. Fire up your test to see the objects that have been persisted, as shown in the following output:

```
// EMPLOYEE Table
ID      NAME
1       Barry Bumbles
2       Harry Dumbles

// EXECUTIVE Table
ID      NAME
2       Director
```

There are two tables, one for each class, unlike the single table in the earlier case that had a discriminating column differentiating the data. The `EXECUTIVE` table has a foreign key pointing to the parent's primary key (in this case, the `id` of the `EMPLOYEE` table).

Table-per-subclass using annotations

We can achieve the same task by using annotations. On the main (parent) class, declare the following annotations:

```
Entity(name="INHERITANCE_S2_EMPLOYEE_ANN")
@Inheritance(strategy= InheritanceType.JOINED)
public class Employee {
  Id
  @Column(name="EMPLOYEE_ID")
  private int id = 0;
  ...
}
```

We set the strategy to table-per-subclass by setting the `InheritanceType` to the `JOINED` value. On the child class, we need to declare its primary join column using `@Primary KeyJoinColumn`, which is the foreign key, as shown here:

```
@Entity(name="INHERITANCE_S2_EXECUTIVE_ANN")
@PrimaryKeyJoinColumn(name="EMPLOYEE_ID")
public class Executive extends Employee
{
  ...
}
```

As expected, two tables will be populated with the employee and executive items once you run the clients.

Next, let's see the third variant of inheritance that Hibernate supports.

Table-per-Concrete-Class Strategy

In the table-per-concrete-class strategy, the object hierarchy is persisted to the individual table for each concrete class. Any properties of the superclass will be copied to the child class's related tables, thus making this strategy uncommon.

Let's see this strategy in action.

We may have to change our object graph a little to fit in a new superclass—the Person class, which is abstract. The Employee and Executive classes extend this superclass and do not extend each other.

The hierarchy is defined in the following snippet:

```
public abstract class Person {
  private int id;
  private String name = null;
  ...
}
public class Employee extends Person{
  private String role = null;
  ...
}
public class Executive extends Person{
  private double bonus = 0.0;
  ...
}
```

Table-per-Concrete-Class Strategy Using XML mapping

The relevant changes to our mapping file are outlined here:

```
<hibernate-mapping package="com.madhusudhan.jh.advanced.inheritance.s3">
  <class name="Person" abstract="true">
    <id  name="id" column="EMPLOYEE_ID">
      <generator class="assigned"/>
    </id>
    <property name="name" column="NAME" />
    <union-subclass name="Employee" table="INHERITANCE_S3_EMPLOYEE">
       <property name="role" column="ROLE"/>
    </union-subclass>
    <union-subclass name="Executive" table="INHERITANCE_S3_EXECUTIVE">
       <property name="bonus" column="BONUS"/>
    </union-subclass>
  </class>
</hibernate-mapping>
```

The Person class, being abstract, is stamped with the abstract="true" property. The id defined by this class is shared across its child classes—therefore, the Employee and Executive class mappings do not mention anything about primary keys.

We tie the subclasses to the parent by using the union-class element. This element declares the child class linking to its own table. Any attributes particular to the child class need to be defined in the union-subclass element, while all the properties defined at the class level are shared by all the children. Note that the native identifier strategy is not allowed in this strategy.

When you run the test client, the data is populated in both tables as expected. In addition to their own properties, the name property (defined in the parent class) will be duplicated in both the tables too. This is one disadvantage of using the table-per-concrete-class strategy.

Table-per-concrete-class strategy using annotations

Last but not least, let's look at how we can model the table-per-concrete-class inheritance strategy using annotations. Although the Person class doesn't have its own persistence table, we may still have to annotate it with @Entity and set its inheritance strategy as TABLE_PER_CLASS. See the Person entity followed by the other two entities here:

```
@Entity
@Inheritance(strategy=InheritanceType.TABLE_PER_CLASS)
public abstract class Person {
  @Id
  @GeneratedValue
  @Column(name="EMPLOYEE_ID")
  private int id;
  ...
}

// Employee class

@Entity(name="INHERITANCE_S3_EMPLOYEE_ANN")
public class Employee extends Person{
    private String role = null;

// Executive class
@Entity(name = "INHERITANCE_S3_EXECUTIVE_ANN")
public class Executive extends Person {
  private double bonus = 0.0;
  ...
}
```

Follow the usual path of enabling the annotated classes in your client and fire up the test client (see earlier examples).

Filters

Sometimes our applications do not need the entire dataset to work with; a subset would be good enough. Take the example of a client interested in finding out all the car models made by a specific company (e.g., Toyota or BMW), or maybe cars by color (red, white, etc.), or by age. It would be a waste of resources if we provided all the Cars to the client and left the client to filter out the irrelevant data.

Hibernate provides a filtering feature for such purposes that acts similarly to SQL's where clause but is more dynamic in nature. You'll see how to use this feature in this section.

There are two steps involved in creating the filters: creating the relevant filter definitions, and enabling them in our code.

Creating Filter Definitions

We define filters using the filter-def element in our mapping file and associate them to each class on which they should be applied. We can define as many filters as we need depending on our requirements. The definition consists of declaring the type of each property that is to be parameterized in our filter query.

Here is an example filter definition:

```
<hibernate-mapping package="com.madhusudhan.jh.advanced.filters">

  <!-- Filter by Make -->
  <filter-def name="filterByMake">
    <filter-param  name="make" type="string"/>
  </filter-def>

  <!-- Filter by color -->
  <filter-def name="filterByColour">
    <filter-param  name="color" type="string"/>
  </filter-def>

  <!-- Filter by Age -->
  <filter-def name="filterByAge">
    <filter-param  name="age" type="integer"/>
  </filter-def>

  <!-- Filter by Make and Model-->
  <filter-def name="filterByMakeAndModel">
    <filter-param  name="make" type="string"/>
    <filter-param  name="model" type="string"/>
  </filter-def>
      ...
</hibernate-mapping>
```

As you can see, this snippet defines four filters. The filter-param declares the name of the column we wish to query. So, in the filterByMake filter, the program is expected to set a parameter with a value against the column name make. The query then transforms to *select * from CARS where make= ?*. The ? is the placeholder to set our search parameter.

We can create as many of these filters in our mapping file as we require. Once we have them defined, we must associate these mapping definitions to our entity definition:

```
<hibernate-mapping package="com.madhusudhan.jh.advanced.filters">
  <filter-def name="filterByMake">
    ...
  </filter-def>
  <class name="Car" table="FILTERS_CAR">
    <id column="CAR_ID" name="id">
      <generator class="native"/>
    </id>
    <property column="COLOR" name="color"/>
    <property column="NAME" name="name"/>
    <property column="MAKE" name="make"/>
    <property column="MODEL" name="model"/>

      <filter name="filterByMake" condition="make = :make"/>
  </class>
</hibernate-mapping>
```

In our class definition, we set the filter using the filter element. It requires two attributes, a name and the condition. The name should match the one we defined in the filter-def definition. The condition follows the same format as our named parameters that we set on the queries. Here's where you define the actual where clause. The :make is the argument that the client needs to set (we will see that in a minute). We don't have to use all the filters; we use only one filter in the preceding case.

Enabling Filters

Let's put this all together and see how we can use the filters:

```
private void test() {
  Filter filter = session.enableFilter("filterByMake");
  filter.setParameter("make", "BMW");
  List results = session.createQuery("from Car").list();
}
```

First, we need to enable the filter by invoking the enableFilter method on the acquired session instance. This method expects the predefined filter name as the argument (filterByMake, in this case). Once we have enabled the filter, the next step is to set the search parameters. From there, you should proceed by using the session instance to create your query and subsequent results.

Relationship Owner (aka Inverse Attribute)

When we are talking about one-to-many or many-to-many relationships, one of the sides should take the responsibility of managing the relationship. In our Movie-Actor example, the Movie mapping is as follows:

```
<class name="Movie" table="MOVIE_ONE2MANY">
  ...
  <set name="actors" table="ACTOR_ONE2MANY" inverse="false" cascade="all">
    <key column="MOVIE_ID" not-null="true"/>
      <one-to-many class="Actor"/>
  </set>
</class>
```

 I know this association is not strictly a one-to-many, as not only can one movie have many actors, but one actor can also star in many movies. For simplicity, however, we'll ignore the latter possibility!

Note that the inverse="false" is actually a default, so you can skip providing the inverse attribute if you wish to set the inverse relationship to false.

In the preceding snippet, as inverse is false, we infer that the relationship is owned by the MOVIES table and not by the ACTORS table. This means that the Movie side is responsible for updating the actor's foreign key MOVIE_ID.

To fulfill this requirement, Hibernate produces three SQL statements: two inserts and one update statement. The two inserts are the statements inserting the data into the MOVIES and ACTORS table, and the update statement updates the relationship in the ACTORS table (i.e., setting the movie_id in the ACTORS table). The third statement is redundant and could be avoided. (That said, it can be suppressed if we set the inverse attribute to true.)

If we set the inverse attribute to true, it works in the opposite way—that is, the ownership lies with the ACTORS table and hence it would maintain the relationship. In this case, only two insert statements are issued—thus eliminating the redundant third update statement, which is good from a performance perspective.

Cascading Entities

When persisting object graphs, we usually have to issue save (or update) commands on individual entities. However, the cascade attribute defined on the graph lets us save the whole graph without our having to worry about saving the entities one by one. The following snippet tries to persist the entities individually:

```
public void nonCascadingSave(){
  ...
  session.saveOrUpdate(movie);
  session.saveOrUpdate(actors);
}
```

However, setting the cascading behavior works in our favor by reducing the lines of code and making it more succinct. We only have to save the parent node; the rest of the graph is handled by Hibernate's runtime.

The cascade attribute is set on the collection attributes, as shown here:

```
<class name="Movie" table="MOVIE_ONE2MANY">
  ...
  <set name="actors" table="ACTOR_ONE2MANY" cascade="save-update"
  inverse="false" >
    <key column="MOVIE_ID" not-null="true"/>
      <one-to-many class="Actor"/>
  </set>
</class>
```

Accordingly, our method reduces to a one-line save statement:

```
public void cascadingSave(){
  ...
  // Movie has all actors!
  session.saveOrUpdate(movie);
}
```

The session.saveOrUpdate(actors) is redundant in this case; the save on the parent Movie object saves the actors automatically.

The same is true for deletion of object graphs too:

```
public void cascadingDelete(){
  ...
  // Remove all the movies AND associated actors!
  session.delete(movie);
}
// XML Mapping
<class name="Movie" table="MOVIE_ONE2MANY">
  ...
  <set name="actors" table="ACTOR_ONE2MANY" cascade="delete" inverse="false" >
    <key column="MOVIE_ID" not-null="true"/>
      <one-to-many class="Actor"/>
  </set>
</class>
```

Setting the cascade attribute to delete will delete the entire movie graph—that is, the movie and its associated actors too.

There is one more case to deal with—a special case called delete-orphan. In our movie/actor example, if we remove the actor from our set collection, delete-orphan would not only dissociate the actor from movie but also delete the actor entity entirely. If this option is not selected, then the movie-to-actor association will be removed, but the actor exists on its own (and is thus an orphan).

```
// XML Mapping
<class name="Movie" table="MOVIE_ONE2MANY">
  ...
  <set name="actors" table="ACTOR_ONE2MANY" cascade="delete-orphan" >
    <key column="MOVIE_ID" not-null="true"/>
      <one-to-many class="Actor"/>
  </set>
</class>
```

Summary

This chapter is a mix of advanced concepts ranging from inheritance, caching, filters, and type system to other important concepts such as inverse and cascading functionality. Understanding these techniques will certainly make you a good Hibernate developer.

CHAPTER 7

Hibernate Query Language

Hibernate introduced its own query language, called the Hibernate Query Language (HQL), specially designed for querying Java object models. It is a simple query language, similar to SQL. We will be using HQL for working on our objects often, so this chapter introduces the features of this query language in detail.

We use Structured Query Language (SQL) to query the relational tables. SQL is the de facto standard when it comes to working with relational databases. However, Hibernate's intent was to create a simple and easy-to-use language to work with object models seamlessly. Hence, in line with SQL, Hibernate created the Hibernate Query Language for querying the Java Object graph. HQL is a simple but powerful feature of the toolkit.

Leveraging developers' familiarity with SQL, the Hibernate team made HQL similar to SQL so the learning curve would be easy. For example, while in SQL we use SELECT * FROM MOVIES to fetch all the records in the MOVIES table, in HQL we'd use FROM Movie. As we are dealing with objects in HQL, we must provide the entity class name that represents our table—in this case, Movie is our persistent Java entity mapped to the MOVIES table. Ideally, we should provide the *fully qualified* name (FQN) of the Movie class, like: FROM com.madhusudhan.jh.hql.Movie. The SELECT statement in HQL is optional if you are querying the entire table's data. However, you must use it when you are working with one or more columns individually, usually called *projections*.

We can use several constructs in HQL—such as WHERE, ORDER BY, AVG, and MAX—just like we do in SQL. We will walk through these bits in this chapter, but first let's look at the fundamental query API.

Working with the Query Class

The Hibernate framework provides a Query API to use with object-relational queries. The Query class, which has a simple interface, forms the centerpiece in this API.

Obviously, the first thing we need to get is an instance of the `Query` before we can do anything meaningful with it. We obtain the instance by calling `createQuery` on a current session object. Once you have the `Query` instance, you can use its methods to get to the result sets obtained from the database.

The following snippet shows how we can get a `Query` instance:

```
// Get the current session
Session session = sessionFactory.getSesion();
// Instance of the query is created from this session
Query query = session.createQuery("from TravelReview");
```

So, we get a session object from our session factory, as expected. Once we have the session object, the next step is to invoke a `session.createQuery` method on it, passing the query we wish to execute in the database. The `createQuery` method accepts a string representation of our query, as shown in the preceding snippet.

Let's see what else is happening here. The `from TravelReview` string is an argument representing a query, equivalent to *get me all the travel reviews from the underlying table*. Accordingly, Hibernate turns this piece of HQL string into a SQL query (databases can only understand SQL queries) and executes it to fetch all rows from a TRAVEL_RE VIEW table. This is similar to the SQL counterpart `SELECT * from TRAVEL_REVIEW`.

However, there are a few subtle differences:

- The `select` keyword is ignored (optional) in HQL if you are selecting the whole table, unlike in SQL.
- While the SQL statement mentions the relation table (`TRAVEL_REVIEW`) in its query, the HQL uses the class's name. The `TravelReview` is the persistent entity representing the table TRAVEL_REVIEW.

Now that we have the `Query` reference obtained from the session, the next step is to use it to fetch the data. This is where we start using the Query API to manipulate the data.

To fetch all the records, we use the query's `list` method, as discussed in the next section.

Fetching All Rows

Fetching all the rows from a table is quite straightforward. The following method fetches all records from our TRAVEL_REVIEW table:

```
private void getAllTravelReviews() {
  Query query = session.createQuery("from TravelReview");
  List<TravelReview> reviews = query.list();
  for (TravelReview travelReview : reviews) {
    System.out.println("Travel Review: " + travelReview);
  }
```

```
      ...
    }
```

Once we have a query instance with the appropriate HQL embedded in it, we invoke the list method to retrieve all the records from the table. Behind the scenes, the Hibernate runtime transforms all the database records into instances of TravelReview and provides them in a java.util.List collection. As this is a standard Java collection, you simply iterate through it to get the individual review (instance) using the for loop shown in the preceding code.

Let's pause for a second and compare this operation against JDBC. While fetching the instances in Hibernate is as easy as writing one or two lines (you can write this in a single line by using chained methods; see the next section), the equivalent in JDBC isn't quite as pleasant. See the following snippet of code to fetch the records using JDBC:

```
private void queryMovies() {
  List<Movie> movies = new ArrayList<Movie>();
  Movie m = null;
  try {
    Statement st = getConnection().createStatement();
    ResultSet rs = st.executeQuery("SELECT * FROM MOVIES");
    while (rs.next()) {
      m = new Movie();
      m.setId(rs.getInt("ID"));
      m.setTitle(rs.getString("TITLE"));
      movies.add(m);
    }
  } catch (SQLException ex) {
    System.err.println(ex.getMessage());
  }
}
```

We create a statement and execute a query on it, which returns a ResultSet instance. This ResultSet instance consists of our records not in object format, but rather in a crude form. We need to run through each ResultSet instance to get the individual row; then, from each individual row, we need to pick the columns either by their name or by the location (we pick them using the column name in the preceding snippet). We then keep creating Movie objects from these bizarrely extracted columns of data and add them to the movies collection. Phew, that was a handful!

By writing just two lines in Hibernate, we've abstracted the whole thing away from us, so we don't have to deal with the low-level stuff anymore. In fact, we can even chain the methods to make this into a one-liner if you wish! For example, instead of instantiating the Query object and invoking the list method on it, you can simply write:

```
List<TravelReview> reviews =
  session.createQuery("from TravelReview").list();
```

That's the power of Hibernate—it takes only one line of code to receive our fully formed collection of Movie objects. Well, Hibernate has more in store when it comes to data queries, so we'll run through a few of these features in the upcoming sections.

Pagination

If we wish to return only a set number of records, we can use the built-in pagination support by invoking setMaxResults with our bounds:

```
Query query =
    session.createQuery("from TravelReview");
query.setMaxResults(100);
query.setFirstResult(10);*
List<TravelReview> reviews = query.list();
```

The setMaxResults method will let Hibernate know that we are interested in seeing only 100 records. There is another option to add to our query—setting the start position of the result set. Where do you want these 100 records to start from—the beginning or from the 10th or 1,000th record? We tune this option by using the setFirstResult method on the query instance. It sets the starting point to the record to be fetched. For example, the preceding code retrieves 100 objects from the table, starting from the 10th record.

Retrieving a Unique Record

When we know there's one and only one record for a query criteria, we could use the API's uniqueResult method. Let's suppose we wish to fetch a travel review for London (expecting one review only for London!). The following query does the job:

```
private void getTravelReviewUniqueRecord() {
    ...
    Query query = session.createQuery("from TravelReview where title='London'");
    TravelReview review = (TravelReview) query.uniqueResult();
}
```

uniqueResult is a convenient method to use when we know that only a single record exists.

Named Parameters

In the previous HQL query, we hardcoded the title to London. We shouldn't be hardcoding any input criteria, however, as the whole point is that this criteria can change often. For example, as a user of a travel site, you may have requested the review of London. But some other user (like me) may request a review of Hyderabad (Hyderabad is a city in southern India, internationally famous for the dish *Hyderabadi biryani*, and where I lived and studied for few years). In both cases, the only thing that changes is the input city name, which should be parameterized. The good news is that we can set input parameters on the Query object using special syntax.

Check out the following snippet:

```
private void getTravelReviewWithQueryParam(String city) {
    ...
  Query query =
    session.createQuery("from TravelReview where title=:titleId");
  query.setString("titleId", city);
}
```

In the preceding example, the :titleId is the placeholder for the input—city name, in this case. The next line sets the value for this placeholder with a required input parameter. We can create as many of the placeholders as required to suit our criteria:

```
Query query = session.createQuery(
  "from TravelReview where title=:titleId and id=:reviewId");

query.setString("titleId", "London");
query.setInteger("reviewId",1);
```

Using the IN option

We may need to fetch data with criteria matching a selective list. For example, say we wish to retrieve the reviews of cities contained in a passed-in parameter list. We need to use HQL's IN option to use this feature. This is equivalent to using SQL's IN operator.

We need a list satisfying our criteria, which we set up using standard Java collection classes. In the next example, we use ArrayList to populate this selective list. We then can use the query's setParameterList method, which accepts the list of items from which our query should fetch:

```
private void getTravelReviewWithQueryParamList() {
{
  ...
  // Define a list and populate with our criteria
  List titleList = new ArrayList();
  titleList.add("London");
  titleList.add("Venice");

  // Construct the query
  Query query =
      session.createQuery("from TravelReview where title in (:titleList)");

  // Notice how we've set the named
  // parameter referring to our titleList?
  query.setParameterList("titleList", titleList);;
  List<TravelReview> reviews =  query.list();
  ...
}
```

Once we have constructed a list of select criteria, we pass it to the query via the `setPar` `ameterList` method. The Hibernate runtime transforms this query into its SQL equivalent:

```
SELECT * from TRAVEL_REVIEW where title in('London','Hyderabad',..)
```

Positional Parameters

Instead of using the named placeholders (prefixing with `:<name>`) as just shown, you can use positional placeholders. Positional placeholders eliminate the string binding of the name/value pairs in a query, instead using integers as their positions. In this case, you use question marks (`?`) as your placeholders. So, the same code from earlier can be rewritten as:

```
Query query =
   session.createQuery("from TravelReview where title=? and id=?");

// title at 0th place
query.setString(0, "London");

// id at 1st place
query.setInteger(1,1);
```

Note that the positional placeholder starts from 0.

 I mentioned positional parameters here, but they have been deprecated in favor of named parameters. Use the named parameter convention whenever you need to set the parameters to your query.

Aliases

Sometimes we wish to give a name to the object we are querying. The names given to tables are called *aliases*, and they are especially helpful when we're constructing joins or subqueries.

The preceding HQL query can be rewritten as shown here:

```
// The tr is the alias to the object
Query query = session.createQuery(
"from TravelReview as tr where tr.title=:title and tr.id=:id"
);
```

Note that the **as** keyword is optional.

Iterators

The `query.list` method returns a list, which in turn returns an iterator. Iterators form an integral part of the Java collection's toolkit, providing the functionality of iterating through a list.

To obtain the iterator, invoke `query.list().iterator` as shown in the following snippet (this method returns `java.util.Iterator` for us to loop through):

```
Query query =
    session.createQuery("from TravelReview");
Iterator queryIter = query.list().iterator();
while(queryIter.hasNext()){
    TravelReview tr = (TravelReview)queryIter.next();
    System.out.println("Travel Review:" + tr);
}
```

As with Java collections, we should use the iterator to delete the item from the underlying collection. We use the `iterator.remove` method to remove an item from the collection.

Selects

The `SELECT` operator in HQL works along the same lines as in SQL(no surprise there!). Should we wish to fetch selected columns from the database (instead of a whole row), we need to use the `SELECT` keyword. It is not case sensitive, so `select` is the same as `SELECT` (it's the same situation with other operators, too!). The list of columns is fetched as a nongeneric list of `Objects`.

For example, if we wish to fetch *only* review descriptions (instead of all of the columns) of all the cities in our table, we would do so as shown here:

```
// The tr is the alias to the object
Query query =
        session.createQuery("SELECT tr.review from TravelReview as tr");

// Each review is a long description in String format
List<String> reviews = query.list();

System.out.println("City Review:");
// Loop through all of the result columns
for (String review : reviews) {
    System.out.println("\t" + review);
}
```

Because we are selecting a single column in the preceding example, we know the expected type. However, when we are selecting multiple columns, how does the query return the result sets? Well, selecting multiple columns results in *tuples*. Tuples are simply an array of objects. The following example selects `title` and `review` in a select query:

```
private void getTravelReviewWithSelectTuples() {
    ...
    String SELECT_QUERY_MULTIPLE_COLUMNS =
    "SELECT tr.title, tr.review from TravelReview as tr";
    Query query = session.createQuery(SELECT_QUERY_MULTIPLE_COLUMNS);
    Iterator reviews = query.list().iterator();
    while(reviews.hasNext()){
        Object[] r = (Object[])reviews.next();
        System.out.print("Title:"+r[0]+"\t");
        System.out.println("Review:"+r[1]);
    }
}
```

The list of returned items is provided as an array of objects. The `title` and `review` are thus retrieved as the first and second elements of the array, respectively, as shown in the preceding snippet.

Expecting and working through tuples isn't elegant. As a more efficient alternative, we can use another feature in Hibernate's toolkit—turning the results into a domain object. For example, let's say we have a `City` instance composed of `title` and `description`. We need to create an instance on every row of data we fetch as follows:

```
String QUERY = "SELECT new City(tr.title, tr.review ) from TravelReview as tr";
// Obtain the cities
List<City> cities = session.createQuery(QUERY).list();
for (City city : cities) {
    System.out.println("City: "+city);
}
```

Did you notice the instantiation of a `City` object in the query itself? `SELECT new City(..)` creates the instances as it loads—quite a convenient way to create brand new incarnations of cities!

Aggregate Functions

Hibernate supports *aggregate* functions such as `avg`, `min`, `max`, and `count(*)` that are equivalent to what SQL provides.

The following snippet is fairly self-explanatory:

```
// Fetching the max ticket price
List review = session.createQuery(
    "select max(ticket_price) from TravelFlight")
    .list();

// Getting the average age of a planet from a galaxy table
List review = session.createQuery(
"select avg(planet_age) from Galaxy")
.list();
```

The max(ticket_price) function returns the maximum price of the flight recorded in the database. Similarly, we calculate the average planet age using the avg aggregate function.

Updates and Deletes

In earlier chapters, we have persisted or updated entities using the session's save (or saveOrUpdate) or delete methods. While we can certainly use them, there's an alternative way to update and delete data: by using the query's executeUpdate method. The method expects a query string with bind parameters, as shown here:

```
// To update the record
String UPDATE_QUERY="update TravelReview set review=:review where id=2";
Query query = session.createQuery(UPDATE_QUERY);
query.setParameter("review", "The city with charm.
The city you will never forget");
int success = query.executeUpdate();
```

The preceding update query uses a bind parameter to set the review for a record whose id=2. The executeUpdate method updates the table and returns an integer indicating if the update was successful. We can use the same method to execute a delete statement:

```
// To delete a record
String DELETE_QUERY="delete TravelReview where id=6";
Query query = session.createQuery(DELETE_QUERY);
int success = query.executeUpdate();
```

Criterias

In earlier sections, we used SQL-based queries using WHERE clauses for our data filtering. Hibernate provides an alternative way of filtering by introducing *criterias*. A criteria is a mechanism through which we set our query conditions on the entity itself. Hibernate provides us a Criteria class along with another class, Restrictions, through which we set the filtering conditions.

Let's fetch a review for London, this time making use of the Criteria and Restrictions classes. Check out the following code example:

```
Criteria criteria =
  session.createCriteria(TravelReview.class);

List review =
  criteria.add(Restrictions.eq("title", "London")).list();

System.out.println("Using equals: " + review);
```

First, we create a Criteria instance from the session and then add Restrictions to it. Restrictions has a few static methods—such as eq (*equals to*), ne (*not equals to*), and like—which are self-explanatory. In the preceding snippet, we fetch all the reviews for a given title, London. Did you notice that we did not use any SQL when obtaining the result set?

We can add restrictions to the criteria by chaining them as follows:

```
Criteria criteria = session.createCriteria(TravelReview.class)
    .add(Restrictions.eq("author", "John Jones"))
    .add(Restrictions.between("date",fromDate,toDate))
    .add(Restrictions.ne("title","New York"));
```

In fact, you could still simplify this without having to have a Criteria class at all, by chaining the list method at the end:

```
List reviews = session.createCriteria(TravelReview.class)
    .add(Restrictions.eq("author", "John Jones"))
    .add(Restrictions.between("date",fromDate,toDate))
    .add(Restrictions.ne("title","New York")).list();
```

The preceding code fetches the reviews for the given selection criteria using object-oriented techniques.

Should we wish to retrieve only a few columns, we can use the Projections class to do so. For example, the following code retrieves the title column from our table:

```
// Selecting all title columns
List review = session.createCriteria(TravelReview.class)
        .setProjection(Projections.property("title"))
    .list();

// Getting row count
review = session.createCriteria(TravelReview.class)
    .setProjection(Projections.rowCount())
    .list();

// Fetching number of titles
review = session.createCriteria(TravelReview.class)
    .setProjection(Projections.count("title"))
    .list();
```

The Projections class has a few other static methods, such as avg (average), row Count (SQL's count(*) equivalent), count (column count), and max and min (maximum and minimum values).

Named Queries

All the while, we have been using the queries in the code itself. Hardcoding the queries isn't a good practice. We have two ways to remove this constraint. We can use the @NamedQuery annotation to bind the queries on the entity at a class level, or we can declare them in our mapping files. In both methods, the named queries are retrieved from the session. Let's check out named queries in action.

When using the annotation route, we need to add the @NamedQuery annotation to our TravelReview entity. The @NamedQuery annotation accepts a name and the query itself, as shown in the following example:

```
@Entity(name="TRAVEL_REVIEW")
@NamedQuery(name = "GET_TRAVEL_REVIEWS",
    query = "from com.madhusudhan.jh.hql.TravelReview")
public class TravelReview implements Serializable {
    ...
}
```

Once we have defined the named query via the annotation, it can be retrieved from the session during runtime. We must use the name attribute to reference the specific named query, as shown in this example:

```
private void usingNamedQueries() {
    ...
    // Fetch the predefined named query
    Query query = session.getNamedQuery("GET_TRAVEL_REVIEWS");
    List reviews = query.list();
}
```

You can also bind multiple queries to an entity by adding each @NamedQuery to a parent @NamedQueries annotation, as shown here:

```
@Entity(name = "TRAVEL_REVIEW")
@NamedQueries(
    value = {
        @NamedQuery(name = "GET_TRAVEL_REVIEWS", query = "from TravelReview"),
        @NamedQuery(name = "GET_TRAVEL_REVIEWS_FOR_TITLE",
        query = "from TravelReview where id=:title")
    }
)
public class TravelReview implements Serializable { ... }
```

@NamedQueries accepts a value argument, which is made up of an array of @Named Query definitions.

When using the declarative path, we should define our queries in our mapping files. For example, we define the travel-related queries in the *TravelReview.hbm.xml* file as follows:

```
<hibernate-mapping>
  <class name="com.madhusudhan.jh.hql.TravelReview" table="TRAVEL_REVIEWS">
    ...
  </class>
  <!-- Define your entity related queries here -->
  <query name="GET_TRAVEL_REVIEWS">
    <![CDATA[ from TravelReview ]]>
  </query>
  <query name="GET_TRAVEL_REVIEWS_FOR_TITLE">
    <![CDATA[ from TravelReview where id=:title ]]>
```

```
    </query
  </hibernate-mapping>
```

The queries should be added in your *hbm* file, associated with the entity class.

Native SQL

Hibernate also provides us with a feature to execute native SQL queries. The `ses sion.createSQLQuery` method returns a `SQLQuery` object, similar to how `create Query` returns a `Query` object. This class extends the `Query` class that we have seen in earlier sections.

As HQL is handy and easy, why bother working with native SQL at all? When we have special queries that might depend upon a database vendor's specific functions or constructs, we use a native SQL strategy. The following snippet illustrates (note, we are not using an exotic SQL query!):

```
SQLQuery query = session.createSQLQuery("select * from NATIVESQL_EMPLOYEE");
List employees = query.list();
```

You may notice that the query string is a properly qualified SQL statement. Note the `SELECT` keyword at the beginning of the query, which is omitted in case of HQL.

As you have just seen in the previous section, you can declare or define native SQL queries outside of the code base. You can employ named queries either by defining the `@NamedQuery` annotation on the entity itself, or by declaring the `sql-query` element in the mapping file. See the following example:

```
<hibernate-mapping>
  <class name="com.madhusudhan.jh.hql.TravelReview" table="TRAVEL_REVIEWS">
    ...
  </class>
  <!-- Define your entity related queries here -->
  <sql-query name="GET_TRAVEL_REVIEWS">
    <![CDATA[ SELECT * from TravelReview ]]>
  </sql-query>
</hibernate-mapping>
```

Inside our program, we need to use the session's `getNamedQuery` method to retrieve the named query. We need to pass in the reference to the named query (in this case, `"GET_TRAVEL_REVIEWS"`), so the `Query` object will be returned.

Summary

In this chapter, you learned the basic workings and important features of the Hibernate Query Language (HQL). HQL is a good add-on to Hibernate's powerful feature set. You have seen HQL used with various options, and how it equates to SQL in general. You also learned about `Criteria` and `Projections` in this chapter.

CHAPTER 8

Java Persistence API

The Java Persistence API (JPA) was developed in order to establish a set of standards for the object-persistence programming world. It was successful in delivering guidelines for ORM persistence providers. Most of the good parts of the JPA specification were derived from Hibernate itself, along with some very well-drawn industry practices, so the specification implementation should not be new to you. The aim of this chapter is to provide you with details about developing JPA-compliant applications using Hibernate.

Standards and specifications make software components easier to port and reuse in disparate environments. They help end users change frameworks without much hassle should they need to do so. The Java community did a good amount of work in enforcing standards by introducing specifications via the Java Community Process (JCP) program.

In the earlier days of the object-relational persistence world, there wasn't any specification for ORM frameworks. We either had to write our own software or work with a nonstandard third-party product, which locked you into the vendor. Most of these frameworks were not generic and robust enough, in the sense that they polluted the architecture knitting the frameworks to the underlying databases. Whether you wrote your own software or went with one of these vendors, it was a big hassle—and in some cases a major headache—to port to another product or database without embarking on a major re-engineering or restructuring project.

Realizing the necessity of a persistence standard, the Java team created the Java Persistence API. In order for a framework to produce standardized and consistent Java persistence software modules, it must adhere to the JPA. Hibernate is one of the frameworks that adopted the specification to produce a good persistence ORM tool. In fact, Hibernate contributed a lot back to the standard with its proven designs.

In this chapter, we will look at Hibernate's support for JPA in detail.

Hibernate and JPA

While JPA is the specification, Hibernate is the implementation provider that follows the rules dictated in the specification. We are already familiar with the Hibernate API classes, such as `Session`, `SessionFactory`, and others. These classes are proprietary to Hibernate (included in the `org.hibernate` package), and hence they're not portable.

So, because Hibernate has to comply with the specification in addition to its own API, it created counterparts to its proprietary API classes, such as the `EntityManager` and `EntityManagerFactory` classes. Unlike its proprietary classes, these classes are included in the `javax.persistence` package. The idea is that if we develop our applications against these JPA classes, should we move away from Hibernate to any other JPA-compliant provider such as EclipseLink, our life should be easy!

Always Use Standards!

When you design a system, consider vendor-free architecture as much as possible. I have seen, over and over again, technical architectures polluted with vendor products and their APIs, which often get us entangled in a mess, unfortunately. Although at times we need to build systems with a certain vendor product's functionality in mind, designing with a clean interface and drawing a line should be always be our first priority. Do not design solutions with vendors in mind; instead, supplement your technical architecture with vendor products and frameworks that support your solution.

I do recommend working with JPA rather than Hibernate's own proprietary API to save yourself a bunch of hassle when you later wish to move away from Hibernate.

From a very broad view, there are only three fundamental bits to working with a JPA-based system. You will learn about them in the coming sections.

Persistence Context

Simply put, the persistence context is a collection of persistent entities. For example, we may have a bunch of entities—such as `Instrument`, `Trade`, and `Security`—against a particular database. We group them all to create a persistence context with the name `trading_entities`, as shown in the following snippet:

```xml
<?xml version="1.0" encoding="UTF-8"?>
<persistence
    xmlns="http://java.sun.com/xml/ns/persistence"
    xmlns:xsi="http://www.w3.org/2001/XMLSchema-instance"
    xsi:schemaLocation="http://java.sun.com/xml/ns/persistence
        http://java.sun.com/xml/ns/persistence/persistence_2_0.xsd"
    version="2.0">
    <persistence-unit name="trading_entities" transaction-type="RESOURCE_LOCAL">
```

```
<provider>org.hibernate.ejb.HibernatePersistence</provider>
    <class>com.madhusudhan.jh.jpa.Instrument</class>
    <class>com.madhusudhan.jh.jpa.Trade</class>
    <class>com.madhusudhan.jh.jpa.Security</class>
    <class>com.madhusudhan.jh.jpa.Risk</class>
    <properties>
      <property name="hibernate.connection.url"
        value="jdbc:mysql://localhost:3307/JH"/>
      <property name="hibernate.connection.driver_class"
        value="com.mysql.jdbc.Driver"/>
      <property name="hibernate.dialect"
        value="org.hibernate.dialect.MySQL5Dialect"/>
      <property name="hibernate.connection.username"
              value="myusername"/>
      <property name="hibernate.connection.password"
              value="mypassword"/>
    </properties>
  </persistence-unit>
</persistence>
```

Here, we first define a `persistence-unit` with the name `trading_entities`. Then, we need to let the runtime know about our JPA implementation provider; in our case, of course, it's Hibernate. We set the `provider` tag with the `org.hibernate.ejb.HibernatePersistence` value to enable Hibernate as our persistence provider. We then declare all our entity classes, one after the other. There are properties defined here, too, which encompass the database connection information that will be used by our provider to connect and access the database.

One important note is that you must place this configuration in a file named *persistence.xml*, which should be placed in the *META-INF* folder. You may have to create this folder at the project level if it doesn't already exist. Make sure to also add the *META-INF* directory to the classpath of your application. The Hibernate JPA runtime browses through the *META-INF* directory to find the *persistence.xml* file for loading and creating the persistence context.

The persistent entities that were present in the persistence unit should be declared with appropriate annotations. You have seen how to create entities using annotations in earlier chapters, but for the sake of review, let's see the `Trade` entity definition with annotations:

```
@Entity
@Table(name="TRADE")
public class Trade {
  @Id
  @Column(name="TRADE_ID")
  private int id = 0;
  ...
}
```

We can define multiple persistence units in the persistence definition file. This comes in handy especially when we have to work with multiple databases. For example, we may have trading-related units talking to MySQL and reporting entities persisted in Oracle. In this case, we define two persistence units, each having the properties specific to its database.

This is shown in the following snippet:

```
<persistence>
  <!-- Persistence unit for MySQL database -->
  <persistence-unit name="trading_entities" transaction-type="RESOURCE_LOCAL">
    <provider>org.hibernate.ejb.HibernatePersistence</provider>
      <class>com.madhusudhan.jh.jpa.Instrument</class>
      <class>com.madhusudhan.jh.jpa.Trade</class>
      <properties>
        <property name="hibernate.connection.url"
          value="jdbc:mysql://localhost:3307/JH"/>
        <property name="hibernate.connection.driver_class"
          value="com.mysql.jdbc.Driver"/>
        ...
  </persistence-unit>

  <!-- Persistence unit for Oracle database -->
  <persistence-unit name="reporting_entities" transaction-type="RESOURCE_LOCAL">
    <provider>org.hibernate.ejb.HibernatePersistence</provider>
      <class>com.madhusudhan.jh.jpa.report.Entity</class>
      <properties>
        <property name="hibernate.connection.url"
          value="jdbc:oracle:thin:@localhost:1521:JH"/>
        <property name="hibernate.connection.driver_class"
          value="oracle.jdbc.driver.OracleDriver"/>
        ...
  </persistence-unit>
</persistence>
```

We have configured separate persistence units for MySQL and Oracle in one configuration file.

What happens to this persistence unit definition and who loads it? Well, there's a utility class called `Persistence`, which looks for *peristence.xml* in the *META-INF* folder inside your classpath. During the runtime, this file is loaded and accordingly the persistence units defined in the file are instantiated.

Once we define the persistence unit, the next step is to look into the `EntityManager Factory` and `EntityManager` classes.

EntityManagerFactory

As the name suggests, `EntityManagerFactory` is a factory class for creating `EntityManagers`. It is a heavy-weight, thread-safe object, and hence for each persistence unit only one instance of the factory is created. Creating this factory is an expensive operation, so the recommended approach is to cache the instance. On the other hand, the Entity Managers created from this factory are safe to use and throw away whenever they're not needed. There will be only one factory created for one persistence unit, but we can have multiple factories, each against a single persistence unit in a single JVM. We obtain a factory from our Persistence instance by passing the persistence unit name, as shown here:

```
// Persistence unit related to trade entities
EntityManagerFactory tradeFactory =
   Persistence.createEntityManagerFactory("trading-entities");

// Persistence unit related to trade entities
EntityManagerFactory reportFactory =
   Persistence.createEntityManagerFactory("report-entities");
```

Two factories, one for the trading entities persistence unit and another for the reporting entities persistence unit, are created as per the preceding code. We can then use them to create EntityManager instances, which act as a gateway to the underlying databases.

Once we have the factory, the next step is to instantiate the EntityManager, which is discussed next.

EntityManager

The EntityManager in every respect is the same as Session: it manages the lifecycle of our entities. It encompasses a unit of work and interacts with the database to work with the entities. It is tied to the current thread of execution for a given transaction and maintains the first level of cache. Once the active transaction to which the EntityMan ager is bound completes, the cache will be recycled.

 Note that the EntityManager is always associated with a persistence context.

There are two types of EntityManagers: one that runs in a container-managed environment, and another in a standalone JVM. The former is typically a Java Enterprise Edition (JEE) container, such as an application server or a web container. The latter is a Java Standard Edition (JSE) standalone program.

There is no difference in EntityManager in either of the ways. However, the EntityMa nagerFactory, which takes the responsibility of creating the EntityManager, is different for both cases. In the container-managed environment, the manager factory will be pre-instantiated (using the configuration bootstrapped) and made available to the application via dependency injection. In a standalone mode, it is the application's responsibility to configure and create the factory.

In a standalone mode, the following procedure demonstrates the method of creating the factory and manager:

```
EntityManagerFactory factory =
    Persistence.createEntityManagerFactory("trading-entities");

EntityManager manager =   factory.createEntityManager();
```

In a container-managed environment on the other hand, the `EntityManager` will be injected by the container. The responsibility of looking up the persistence unit, creating the factory, and subsequently creating and injecting the `EntityManager` is left to the JEE application container.

As the entity is annotated with an `@Resource` annotation (see the following listing), the pre-instantiated `EntityManager` instance will be readily available for injection.

```
@Resource
private EntityManager manager = null;
```

Once we have the manager at our disposal, we can see the JPA workings.

Persisting Objects

Similar to Hibernate's persistence model, JPA exposes its own API for helping developers working with persistence. `EntityManager` is the class that we will focus on, as it is the primary door to the database.

Saving and Querying Entities

We use session's `save` and `saveOrUpdate` methods to persist the entities to the database. Parallel to this functionality, we use `EntityManager`'s `persistEntity` method to save the object in a database in JPA mode.

This is illustrated in the following example:

```
public void persistNewInstrument(){
    // Create the entity manager
    EntityManager manager = entityManagerFactory.createEntityManager();

    // Create and populate the instrument object
    Instrument instrument = new Instrument();
    instrument.setIssue("IBM");

    // Save the domain object
    manager.persist(instrument);
```

We search for and retrieve the objects via the `getReference` method, as shown here:

```
public void findInstrument() {
  Instrument instrument = manager.getReference(Instrument.class,1);
}
```

The preceding method takes two arguments: the domain class itself and a primary key.

There's also a find method to retrieve the object, which is similar to the aforementioned getReference method. This is shown in the following snippet:

```
public void findInstrument() {
  Instrument instrument = manager.find(Instrument.class,1);
}
```

However, there are a few subtle differences between these two approaches. getRefer ence fetches a lazy-loaded entity. This means that the attributes of the class, apart from its primary key, are not fetched (hence, they would be null) until we access them. The find method, on the other hand, does the opposite. Also, the getReference method throws an EntityNotFoundException if there's no record in the database, while the find method simply returns a null value.

Deleting entities is simple too. Using the EntityManager's remove method, we can delete the entities from our durable storage:

```
public void deleteInstrument() {
    manager.remove("IBM");
}
```

We use the flush and refresh methods to synchronize the state of the persistent entities with the database. The flush method updates the database with the modified copies of the objects, while refresh does the opposite: it updates the object model with the latest copy of the records, reading from the database.

This concludes our high-level tour of JPA and Hibernate in this chapter.

Summary

The Java Persistence API (JPA) sets the standards for the Java persistence world. In this chapter, you learned the basics of JPA and skimmed through the APIs. You learned that Hibernate supports the JPA fully, and we should try to plug into the JPA APIs whenever possible, or when we know we need to make our code portable.

Index

Symbols

== operator, 19
@Cascade annotation, 53
@Column annotation, 32
   setting more options for each column, 34
   specifying column name, 33
@DiscriminatorColumn annotation, 82
@DiscriminatorValue annotation, 82
@Embeddable annotation, 36, 37
@EmbeddedId annotation, 37
@Enity annotation, 67
@Entity annotation, 21, 32, 53
@GeneratedValue annotation, 34
@Id annotation, 21, 32, 67
   embedding primary key class on persisten
     class's id variable, 36
@IdClass annotation, 38
@Inheritance annotation, 81
@JoinColumn annotation, 53, 67
@JoinTable annotation, 55
@NamedQuery annotation, 102
@OneToMany annotation, 53
@OneToOne annotation, 67
@PrimaryKeyJoinColumn annotation, 84
@SequenceGenerator annotation, 35
@Table annotation, 21, 33, 53
@TableGenerator annotation, 35

A

accessor methods, using annotations on, 32
addAnnotatedClass method, Configuration
   class, 33
aggregate functions, 100
AJOs (annotated Java objects), 20
   POJOs versus, 39
aliases, 98
annotations, 21, 31–40
   @Column, 33
   @NamedQuery, 102
   @Table, 33
   ID generation strategies using, 34
   making Employee class persistent (example),
     32
   setting composite-id identifiers, 36
     using primary key class and @Embedde-
       dId, 37
     using primary key class and @Id, 36
   using in one-to-one association, 66
   using in table-per-class strategy, 81
   using in table-per-concrete-class strategy, 86
   using in table-per-subclass inheritance strat-
     egy, 84
   using on class variables versus accessor
     methods, 32
   using to persist collections, 52–55
array element, 49

We'd like to hear your suggestions for improving our indexes. Send email to index@oreilly.com.

arrays
    of objects, 99
    persisting, 49
as keyword, 98
Assigned class, 27
assigned strategy, 26
associations, 19, 57–72
    bidirectional one-to-many, 70
    directionality, 59
        bidirectional, 59
        unidirectional, 59
    inverse attribute, 89
    many-to-many, 71
    multiplicity, 58
    one-to-many, 67–70
    one-to-one, 60
        annotations, 66
        using a foreign key, 64
        using a primary key, 61
    representing in Java, 57
    types of, with definition and example, 59
AUTO ID generation strategy, 34
avg function, 101

B

bag element, 50
bags, 50
basic types, 74
BasicMovieManager application (example), 7
    creating persist method, 12
    creating SessionFactory class for, 11
    fetching all moves from the database table, 13
    testing persisted data with findMovie method, 13
BasicType interface, 74
bidirectional associations, 59
    many-to-many, 71
    many-to-many bidirectional association, 60
    one-to-many bidirectional association, 70
    one-to-one bidirectional association, 60
business key, 36

C

cache attribute, class element, 78
CacheProvider interface, 78
caching, 77
    first-level, 77

queries, 79
    second level, 78
cascade attribute
    delete, 90
    delete-orphan, 91
    save-update, 90
cascading entities, 89
class-to-table mapping definitions, 11, 25
classes
    annotated, letting Hibernate configuration
        know about, 33
    annotations, 31
    attributes (variables), representing associa-
        tions, 57
Collection interface, 41
collections, 41–55
    designing to interfaces, 41
    lists, 95
    persisting arrays, 49
    persisting bags and idbags, 50
        bags, 50
        idbags, 51
    persisting lists, 42
        car showroom (example), 42
        testing persistence, 44
    persisting maps, 47
        testing persistence, 48
    persisting sets, 45
        testing persistence, 46
    persisting using annotations, 52
        using a foreigh key, 52
        using a join table, 54
column tag, 25
columns
    @Column annotation, 32
    column name matching variable name of an
        object, 25
com.mysql.jdbc.Driver class, 3
component element, 77
component type, 74
components, 75
composite identifiers, 36
    creating using @IdClass, 38
    creating using primary key class and @Em-
        beddedId, 37
    creating using primary key class and @Id, 36
composite or compound key, 36
Configuration class, 24

configuration files
    annotated classes, 33
    for database connections in Hibernate, 9
    hibernate.cfg.xml or hibernate.properties
        file, 22
    mapping files and their locations in Hiber-
        nate, 10
    referencing mapping file in, 26
    using an XML file, 23
Configuration object, 12
    chaining methods on, 33
configuration properties, 23
configuration, programmatic, 23
Criteria class, 101
criterias, 101
custom types, 74

D

database connections
    configuring in Hibernate applications, 8
    creating using JDBC, 3
databases, 2, 14
    field names, 32
    hibernate.properties file for different databa-
        ses, 22
    identity function, 34
    mapping objects to tables, 24
    SessionFactory for, 10
    setting up MySQL, 15
datatypes
    Hibernate types, 73
        custom types, 74
        entity and value types, 73
    of object attributes, 25
dependencies, Hibernate dependencies in
    pom.xml file, 14
Derby database
    connection properties in hibernate.proper-
        ties file, 22
    EmbeddedDriver class, 3
development environment, setting up, 14
directionality (in associations), 59
discriminator column, 79
    defining with @DiscriminatorColumn anno-
        tation, 82
domain model, 17
domain objects, 17
download site for supplemental material, xiv
Driver class, 3

driver classes, 22

E

EhCache, 78
Employee class (example), 31
    annotating with @Column, 32
    annotating with @Entity, 32
    annotating with @Id, 32
    annotating with @Table, 33
entity types, 73
equal objects, 19
equals method, 19, 36, 38
    implementing for sets, 46
exceptions, persisting entities to the database, 29

F

filter element, 88
filters, 87
    creating filter definitions, 87
    enabling, 88
foreign generator class, 63
foreign key, 58
    in CARS_SET table (example), 46
    using in car showroom (example), using
        @JoinColumn annotation, 53
    using in one-to-one association, 64
    using in table-per-subclass inheritance strat-
        egy, 83
    using to persist collections, 52
fully qualified name (FQN), 93

G

generator attribute, @GeneratedValue annota-
    tion, 34
generator class, 26
GeneratorType values, 35

H

has-a relationship, 18, 79
hashCode method, 36, 38
    implementing for sets, 46
HashSet class, 45
.hbm.xml file extension, 24
hbm2ddl.auto property, 15
Hibernate framework, xi
    birth of, 1

caching, 77
    caching queries, 79
    first-level, 77
    second-level, 78
cascading entities, 89
components, 75
configuration, 22
    programmatic, 23
    using hibernate.properties file, 22
configuration properties, 23
configuring the database connection, 9
creating an application, steps to follow, 8
creating mapping definitions file, 10
filters, 87
identifier generation strategies, 26
inheritance
    table-per-concrete-class strategy, 85
    table-per-subclass strategy, 83
main parts, 19
mapping, 24
mapping files and their locations, 10
persistent classes, 20
persisting Movie instance to a database, 7
persisting objects, 11
problem domain, 3
Query API, 93
relationship owner, 89
Session APIs, 27
setting up, 14
testing persisted data, 13
trading application (example), 20
transactions, 28
types, 73
    custom types, 74
    entity and value types, 73
using annotations, 20
    mapping ID field from EMPLOYEE table
        to id variable on Employee class, 32
version 4.2, 12
Hibernate Query Language (HQL), 93–104
    executing native SQL queries, 104
    working with the Query class, 93
        aggregate functions, 100
        criterias, 101
        fetching all rows, 94
        iterators, 99
        named parameters, 96
        pagination, 96
        positional parameters, 98
        retrieving a unique record, 96
        selects, 99
        updates and deletes, 101
        using aliases, 98
        using the IN option, 97
hibernate-mapping element, 11
hibernate.cfg.xml file, 9
    declaring annotated class in, 33
    hbm2ddl.auto property, 15
hibernate.properties file, 9
    database connection properties, 22
HibernateException, 29
Hyderabad, 96

I

id tag, 25
    generator class for, 26
idbags, 51
idbags element, 52
identical objects, 19
IdentifierGenerator interface, 27
identifiers
    @Id annotation, 32
    composite, 36
        creating using @IdClass, 38
        creating using primary key class and
            @Embedded, 37
        setting using primary key class and @Id,
            36
    generating object identifiers automatically,
        26
    generation strategies using annotations, 34
    object ID, mapping to primary key of a table,
        25
identity function, 34
identity mismatch, 2, 18
identity of an object, 20
identity strategy, 27
IDENTITY strategy, 34
IDEs, 14
IN option (HQL), 97
InfiniSpan, 78
inheritance, 2
    is-a relationship, not understood by relation-
        al databases, 79
    not supported by relational model, 18
    table-per-class strategy, 79
        using annotations, 81
        using XML mapping, 80

table-per-concrete-class strategy, 85
    using annotations, 86
    using XML mapping, 85
table-per-subclass strategy, 83
    using annotations, 84
    using XML mapping, 83
InheritanceType, 82
    JOINED value, 84
interfaces, collection, 41
inverse attribute, 89
is-a relationship, 79
iterators, 99

J

Java, 1
    reflection, 26, 73
java.io.Serializable interface, 36
java.util.Collection interface, 41
java.util.List interface, 41, 95
java.util.Map interface, 41
java.util.Set interface, 41
JavaDB, 22
    (see also Derby database)
    JDBC connection class, 3
javax.persistence package, 21
JBoss, InfiniSpan, plugging in as cache provider, 78
JDBC (Java Database Connectivity), 2
    creating database connection, 3
    fetching all rows, 95
JDK 5.0+, 14
join table, 54
joined-class element, 84
JPA (Java Persistence API) annotations, 21

L

list element, 43
lists
    java.util.List collection, 95
    List collection of cars in showroom (example), 53
    List interface, 41
    persisting, 42
        car showroom (example), 42
        testing the persistence, 44
    returning List of all movies (example), 13
load method, Session object, 13

M

many-to-many associations, 19, 58, 71, 89
    many-to-many bidirectional association, 60
many-to-one associations (see one-to-many associations)
many-to-one element, 65, 70
map element, 48
Map interface, 41
mapping
    in array persistence (example), 49
    in list persistence (example), 43
    in one-to-one association using a primary key, 62
    in persisting maps (example), 48
    in set persistence (example), 46
    of persistent classes using XML files, 31
    table-per-class strategy using XML mapping, 80
    table-per-concrete-class strategy using XML mapping, 85
    table-per-subclass strategy using XML mapping, 83
mapping element, using to declare annotated class, 33
mapping files, 20, 24
    creating filters in, 88
    declaring sql-query element, 104
    defining named queries in, 103
    Movie.hbm.xml file (example), 10
    referencing in configuration file, 26
    XML files
        Trade.hbm.xml (example), 24
        with .hbm.xml extension, 24
maps
    choice for key/value-paired data, 47
    persisting, 47
        testing persistence, 48
Maven, creating Maven project in NetBeans, 14
max function, 101
Movie.hbm.xml mapping file (example), 10
MovieManager application (example), 3
    creating SQL statements and executing them, 5
    Java-Hibernate version, developing, 8
    persisting the Movie object, 6
    persistMove and queryMovie methods, 4
    using JDBC, 3
MoviePersistor class (example), 6

multiplicity (in associations), 58
  one-to-one bidirectional association, 60
MySQL, 14
  class for JDBC database connection, 3
  database connection configuration files in
    Hibernate, 9
  setting up, 15

N

name attribute, class tag, 11
named queries, 102, 104
NetBeans IDE, 14
  creating Maven project in, 14
nullable attribute, @Column annotation, 34

O

object associations, 2
object model, converting to relational model, 6
object-oriented languages, 2
object-relational impedance mismatch, 2, 17
  inheritance mismatch, 18
  object-relational impedance mismatch, 18
  relations and associations mismatch, 19
object-relational mapping (ORM), 1
  birth of ORM tools, 19
  converting POJO to a database row, 7
  Hibernate as tool for, 2
  mapping files in Hibernate, 10
objects, 1
  arrays of, 99
  associations between (see associations)
  creating plain old Java object (POJO), 6
  identifiers, generating automatically, 26
  identity, 20
  individual mappings per object in class ele-
    ment, 11
  inheritance, 18
  mapping to database tables, 24
  POJOs versus AJOs, 39
  unique identifier for, 11
one-to-many associations, 19, 58, 89
  bidirectional, 70
  example using Actor and Movie classes, 67–
    70
  Showroom class with cars (example), 43
one-to-one associations, 19, 58
  example using Car and Engine classes
    annotations, 66

example, using Car and Engine classes, 60
  testing, 63
  using a foreign key, 64
  using a primary key, 61
one-to-one bidirectional association, 60
one-to-one tag, 62
  constrained attribute, 63
org.hibernate.cache.spi.CacheProvider interface, 78
org.hibernate.id.Assigned class, 27
org.hibernate.id.IdentifierGenerator interface,
  27
org.hibernate.SessionFactory class, 27
org.hibernate.type.BasicType interface, 74

P

pagination support (Query class), 96
param elements, 27
persistence, 1
  creating persist method in BasicMovieMan-
    ager class (example), 12
  method persisting a move, refactored
    through Hibernate, 7
  persisting collections, 41–55
  persisting objects with Hibernate, 11
  persisting POJO object into database table, 6
  testing persisted data, 13
persistent classes, 20
persistent entities, 32
POJOs (plain old Java objects), 6, 20
  versus AJOs, 39
positional placeholders, 98
PreparedStatement object, 5
primary key, 19, 58
  generation by database with Hibernate AU-
    TO strategy, 34
  object identifier mapped to, 25
  setting composite-id identifiers with primary
    key class and @Id, 36
  TRADE_ID column of TRADES table (ex-
    ample), 20
  using in one-to-one association, 61
projections, 93
Projections class, 102
properties in hibernate.properties file, 9
property tag, 25

Q

Query class, 93
  fetching all rows, 94
  getting a Query instance, 94
  named queries, 102
  obtaining an iterator, 99
  pagination support with setMaxResults
    method, 96
  retrieving a unique record, 96
  selects, 99
  setCacheable method, 79
  setting input parameters, 97
  updates and deletes using executeUpdate
    method, 101
  using aggregate functions, 100
  using aliases, 98
  using positional parameters, 98
  using the IN option, 97
Query objects, 13

R

reflection, 26, 73
relational databases, 1
  and object-relational mismatch, 18
  programmed with object-oriented languages, 2
  querying with SQL, 93
  relationships between database tables, 58
relationships, 2
  defined, 58
resource attribute, 10
Restrictions class, 101
ResultSet object, 95

S

schema, creating, 15
select keyword in HQL, 94
SELECT operator in HQL and SQL, 99
SELECT statement, 5
  in HQL, 93
  running SELECT * FROM MOVIES (example), 13
  SELECT * from TRAVEL_REVIEW, 94
sequence strategy, 27
  defining strategy and sequence generator, 35
Serializable interface, 36
ServiceRegistry class, 12

Session APIs, 27
Session objects, 10, 28
  beginTransaction method, 29
  createQuery method, 13, 94
  createSQLQuery method, 104
  load method, 13
  persisting Movie object using session.save
    method (example), 13
  transactional cache associated with, 77
SessionFactory class, 10, 27
  creating, 11
  creating using properties in XML configuration file, 23
  initializing using pre-4.x version of Hibernate, 12
  second-level cache available via, 78
Set interface, 41
set tag, 45
sets
  persisting, 45
    satisfying equality requirement, 46
    testing persistence, 46
    using HashSet as Set implementation, 45
SQL (Structured Query Language), 93
SQL queries
  executing native SQL queries in Hibernate, 104
  running query to test persisted data, 13
SQL statements
  predefined, 5
  where clause, 87
sql-query element, 104
SQLQuery object, 104
strategy attribute, @GeneratedValue annotation, 34
supplemental material, download site, xiv

T

table attribute, class tag, 11, 25
table-per-class strategy, 79
  using annotations, 81
  using XML mapping, 80
table-per-concrete-class strategy, 85
  using annotations, 86
  using XML mapping, 85
table-per-subclass strategy, 83
  using annotations, 84
  using XML mapping, 83

trading application (example)
    identifiers for Trade POJOs, 20
    Trade object mapping in Trade.hbm.xml file, 24
    Trade POJOs, identity and equality comparisons, 18
    using annotations, 21
Transaction objects, creating, 29
transactions, 10
    ACID properties, 28
    fetching, 29
    Session and Transaction objects, 28
tuples, 99
type safety, not imposed by XML mapping files, 31
type tag, 25
types (see datatypes; Hibernate framework, types)

U

unidirectional associations, 59
union-subclass element, 86

unique attribute, @Column annotation, 34
unordered collections, 50
usage attribute, cache element, 78

V

value types, 73
    basic types, 74
    components, 74
VM (virtual machine) arguments, 24

W

web page for this book, xv
where clause (SQL), 87, 88

X

XML files
    Hibernate configuration, 23
    hibernate.cfg.xml, 9
    mapping files, 24
    mappings of persistent classes, 31

About the Author

Madhusudhan Konda is an experienced Java consultant working in London, primarily with investment banks and financial organizations. Having worked in enterprise and core Java for the last 12 years, he is interested in distributed, multithreaded, *n*-tier scalable, and extensible architectures. He is experienced in designing and developing high-frequency and low-latency application architectures. He enjoys writing technical papers and is interested in mentoring.

Colophon

The animal on the cover of *Just Hibernate* is a garden dormouse (*Eliomys quercinus*), a rodent in the dormouse family. Garden dormice grow to about 3.9–5.9 in (10–15 cm) in length not counting the tail, which can add up to 3–5.7 in (8–14.5 cm). They weigh from 2–5 oz (60–140 g). Their outer coat is gray brown and they have a white underside. The garden dormouse is recognizable by its black eye markings, large ears, short hair, and white tassel at the end of its tail.

Garden dormice mostly live in the forest, despite the name, found throughout southern Europe—the Alps, the Bavarian Forest, and the Ore Mountains. The species can also be found in small quantities in northern Germany and is nearly extinct in the Netherlands, where in 2007, researchers reported finding only nine dormice in two woods in Limburg where species used to be common.

The species is nocturnal and sleeps in spherical nests in trees during the day. They hunt for food at night, feeding mostly on large insects like grasshoppers and beetles, snails, eggs, small rodents, spiders, and vegetation such as berries, fruit, and nuts. They consume slightly more animal protein than vegetation.

Garden dormice mate from April to June. The female squeaks loudly, indicating she is ready to mate. During mating season, it is not unusual for a dormouse to eat a rival in the mating process. There is also occasional cannibalism noted when dormice are coming out of hibernation. Gestation periods are about 23 days, and young are born in litters of 3 to 7. Another 18 days after birth, the young open their eyes and are nursed until they are one month old. At two months, they are independent, and within a year after birth, they are sexually mature. A garden dormouse usually lives up to five years.

The cover image is from *Lydekker's Royal Natural History*. The cover fonts are URW Typewriter and Guardian Sans. The text font is Adobe Minion Pro; the heading font is Adobe Myriad Condensed; and the code font is Dalton Maag's Ubuntu Mono.

Have it your way.

O'Reilly eBooks

- Lifetime access to the book when you buy through oreilly.com

- Provided in up to four, DRM-free file formats, for use on the devices of your choice:
  PDF, .epub, Kindle-compatible .mobi, and Android .apk

- Fully searchable, with copy-and-paste, and print functionality

- We also alert you when we've updated the files with corrections and additions.

oreilly.com/ebooks/

Safari Books Online

- Access the contents and quickly search over 7000 books
  on technology, business, and certification guides

- Learn from expert video tutorials, and
  explore thousands of hours of video
  on technology and design topics

- Download whole books or chapters
  in PDF format, at no extra cost,
  to print or read on the go

- Early access to books as they're being written

- Interact directly with authors of upcoming books

- Save up to 35% on O'Reilly print books

See the complete Safari Library at safari.oreilly.com

©2014 O'Reilly Media, Inc. O'Reilly logo is a registered trademark of O'Reilly Media, Inc. 14373

Get even more for your money.

Join the O'Reilly Community, and register the O'Reilly books you own. It's free, and you'll get:

- $4.99 ebook upgrade offer
- 40% upgrade offer on O'Reilly print books
- Membership discounts on books and events
- Free lifetime updates to ebooks and videos
- Multiple ebook formats, DRM FREE
- Participation in the O'Reilly community
- Newsletters
- Account management
- 100% Satisfaction Guarantee

Signing up is easy:

1. Go to: oreilly.com/go/register
2. Create an O'Reilly login.
3. Provide your address.
4. Register your books.

Note: English-language books only

To order books online:
oreilly.com/store

For questions about products or an order:
orders@oreilly.com

To sign up to get topic-specific email announcements and/or news about upcoming books, conferences, special offers, and new technologies:
elists@oreilly.com

For technical questions about book content:
booktech@oreilly.com

To submit new book proposals to our editors:
proposals@oreilly.com

O'Reilly books are available in multiple DRM-free ebook formats. For more information:
oreilly.com/ebooks

©2014 O'Reilly Media, Inc. O'Reilly logo is a registered trademark of O'Reilly Media, Inc. 14373

Lightning Source UK Ltd.
Milton Keynes UK
UKHW031833250123
415958UK00007B/349